WE BELONG

TOGETHER

CHURCHES

in Solidarity with

WOMEN

Solidarity belongs to the faith.
We speak in terms of unity and community;
we call ourselves families and communions.
We believe that we belong together,
that as the church we are one body
and when one part suffers all suffer
and the gift of each is the asset of the whole.

Mercy Oduyoye
Who Will Roll the Stone Away?

WE BELONG
TOGETHER

CHURCHES
in Solidarity with
WOMEN

Edited with introductions by
Sarah Cunningham

FRIENDSHIP PRESS • NEW YORK

Unless otherwise noted, Bible quotations are from the New Revised
Standard Version, copyright © 1989 by the Division of Education and
Ministry of the National Council of the Churches of Christ in the U.S.A.
Used by permission.

Friendship Press and the editor are grateful to several publishers for
permission to reprint articles, excerpts from articles, and a poem. Sources
are cited with each reprinted selection. Full credits and permission are
cited in the Acknowledgments, page 132.

Copyright © 1992 by Friendship Press

Editorial Offices:
475 Riverside Drive, Room 860, New York, NY 10115

Distribution Offices:
P.O. Box 37844, Cincinnati, OH 45222-0844

All rights reserved. No part of this book may be reproduced in any
manner whatsoever without written permission of the publisher, except
brief quotations embodied in critical articles or reviews.

Manufactured in the United States of America

Library of Congress Cataloging-in-Publication Data
We belong together : churches in solidarity with women / edited
by Sarah Cunningham.
    p.   cm.
Includes bibliographical references.
ISBN 0-377-00242-9
    1. Women in Christianity.   I. Cunningham, Sarah, 1925–
BV639.W7W4   1992
261.8'344–dc20
                                           92-7553
                                               CIP

Contents

Preface

Many of us who grew up in the first half of the twentieth century in North American societies had such benevolent and supportive fathers, mothers, pastors and teachers that we rarely questioned the traditional patterns of home and church.

Pastors were always men, as were almost all elders, deacons, stewards, trustees and other lay leaders of official church boards. Church school teachers — at least for children — were usually women. Women also were organized for mission, and in smaller, particularly rural churches, it was usually the women who "kept things going." Still, the major authority figures of "the church" at every level were men. All this led to a kind of uneasy and irrational, but nevertheless rarely questioned, assumption that men and women were "equal but different," with the ultimate authority to decide what that meant still in the hands of men.

We had a subliminal awareness that women were considered a little lower than men on the ladder of reality. But somehow, our rung was a fairly comfortable, "supportive" place to be, with many advantages attached so that we hardly noticed. Men and women had different functions in the social order. And in this world of paradox, it was a fairly common assumption that women understood men better than men understood women; therefore, women could "make allowances" and "be there for their men." But perhaps even then there was already brewing in the minds of many fathers (mothers had known it all along) the idea that their daughters were in every way equal to their sons, and since neither sons nor daughters now had to have the physical strength to clear the forest before they could build a home, things would have to change.

For the time being, however, girls were still taught that boys took the initiative in the mating game, proposing the marriage, providing engagement ring and wedding band. Wearing a wedding band was optional for the man, but not for the woman. The ring was an assumed sign of having been "taken" in marriage. The wife was to take her husband's name, giving up her own surname, and the family was to be known as his family. He would be the head of the household and provide the income. She would bear the children and keep the house. The primary requirement for young girls was that they be at least "pretty" if not "beautiful." Intellectual achievement could be left to the boys.

As we moved on into the century, it became all right for girls to achieve academically and professionally, but the real rewards still came in being beautiful, and later in "keeping house," eventually upgraded to "homemaking." And though it sounds like a contradiction in assumptions about who was in charge, if difficulties ever arose in marriages, it was the responsibility of women to work things out. All the "good housekeeping" magazines of the day offered advice on how to do this, 90 percent of the task being that of the woman.

But There Were Other Realities

The benevolent patriarchal society was still a part of this century's white, middle- and upper-class reality well into the 1950s and 1960s. But other realities existed as well. The World War, followed by the Korean and Vietnam wars, the civil rights movement and the general restlessness of peoples who had lost their innocence were all prelude to the women's liberation movement of the late 1960s, gaining momentum in the 1970s.

Many families and neighborhoods had been thwarted throughout the century by race, class and economic factors. Women of entire races, for instance, could be considered "not beautiful" by the dominant culture. So how could they possibly experience the American dream, warped as it was, as imaged for them in the popular media of the day? Recently, a television retrospective of the United States of World War II included the ever-present "pin-up girls" in the military barracks. No African American, Latina, Indian or Asian images were among them. In fact, it was hard to find a man, woman or child other than white in the whole retrospective of what we, as U.S. citizens, were "remembered" to be like in those days.

The experience of Americans of color in this and previous centuries was another story altogether. Women (or men, for that matter) of color did not experience patriarchy on the part of white men as benevolent. And given recent statistics to the effect that 40 percent of all women in the United States have experienced serious sexual abuse (either physical or psychological) from other family members,[1] even our perception of the dominant twentieth-century family culture is no doubt only a surface reality.

The Canadian reality was different in detail from any of these briefly sketched images, but the issues were basically the same. At any rate, it is probably safe to assume that prior to World War II, only a select number of women of any racial or ethnic group on this continent had a highly developed consciousness of why women so often felt unfulfilled in their roles as women.

In the last half of this century, following the explosive, energizing ferment of the women's liberation movement, more and more women began to do serious research in all fields of knowledge affecting their self-definition, including biblical interpretation and church practices and traditions. We have begun to look with a very critical eye at all the assumptions that have shaped our thinking, our life choices, our religious expressions.

Delving into the past, many of us have been shocked to discover also that some women had been doing historical research and critical analysis for generations. Neither their names nor their findings had been introduced to us when we were supposedly receiving a liberal arts education.

Enlightened, courageous women have spoken out in every generation against second-class citizenship and oppression. But that knowledge was not consistently and widely shared in our places of learning so that we could use it to effect needed change. And as long as many women lived in relationships that were basically comfortable and hospitable to their functions as wives, mothers, supporters of the status quo — as teachers, nurses, maids, cooks and the like — little change was likely to happen. Even those who lived in abusive circumstances had no voice or power to bring about change.

But in every generation, the number of women who could not easily adapt to the status quo has increased. The multimedia explosion of the last thirty years has made a tremendous contribution to the visibility of women's issues, whether in regard to physical and psychological violence, unequal distribution of labor and pay, exploitation of women's bodies in advertising, governmental control of women's reproductive rights or the co-optation of women in general — in every field. As more and more women began to speak out about their experiences and dreams, it became obvious that the "ideal" arrangement of benevolent, providing father and altruistic,

---

1. Diana Russell, *The Secret Trauma: Incest in the Lives of Girls and Women* (New York: Basic Books, 1986).

giving, stay-at-home mother was a very simplistic image of a much more complex reality.

The Pyramid Can't Define Us Anymore

The church has traditionally visualized the divine/human order as a pyramid with God (imaged as male) at the top; men as fathers, authority figures and providers on the next level down; then women as wives and mothers; children next; and finally animals and plants at the lowest level. The theology that made God male, and man next in the line of descent, worked hand in hand with a patriarchal family structure. Such an arrangement may have even been necessary at one stage in the development of civilization, but it led to excessive male control of women and children at other stages. Now we are recognizing the total inadequacy of such a system for this or future generations.[2]

Our biblical ancestors seem to have viewed the universe as a three-tiered world of heaven, earth and hell. Today we see the world quite differently. Scientists talk of a relational universe, where out of continuing chaos come orderly arrangements and rearrangements, a universe where everything relates to everything else, a universe in which even those things we call "solid" are made up of continuously interacting parts. Such a different view of the world calls for a new approach also to the way we talk about ultimate realities, about religious meanings, about God and neighbor. And about human beings as male and female.

This book reflects on some of the beliefs and patterns of the past that have alienated women and men from each other in the life of the church. It also takes note of changes that have already begun to alter the way we think about and express our faith — both in the way we worship and the way we act. The reflections gathered here offer waystations on a journey already begun, brief roadside views of what lies behind us and before us as well as at the surrounding scene.

We hope that local churches will more and more be the setting where women and men come together to discuss the implications of these changes and that this book will be useful in those shared explorations of what equality and inclusiveness require. We belong together for the sake of the church and the world.

---

2. See Alice L. Hageman, ed., *Sexist Religion and Women in the Church: No More Silence* (New York: Association Press, 1974). Also, Nelle Morton, *The Journey Is Home* (Boston: Beacon Press, 1985).

FEMINISTS AND WOMANISTS

Two words that will appear from time to time in this book are "feminist" and " womanist."

"Feminist" (or its derivative, "feminism") is a word that has taken on pejorative meanings for some people, but in its original use and still today it simply stands for those who believe in the equality of women and men and who are willing to live by their convictions. Men as well as women can be feminists.

"Womanist" is a term first popularized for an interracial audience by poet and author Alice Walker in her book In Search of Our Mothers' Gardens *(New York: Harcourt Brace, 1983) and quoted by Delores Williams in an article titled "Womanist Theology: Black Women's Voices," that appeared in the March 2, 1987, issue of* Christianity and Crisis. *Williams adds, "A womanist is a black feminist or feminist of color. A womanist is committed to survival and wholeness of an entire people, male and female.... Womanist theology, a vision in its infancy, is emerging among Afro-American women."*

Through a collection of writings, some solicited especially for this book, others excerpted from a variety of sources, we will explore this theme of "The Churches in Solidarity with Women" from the perspectives of Tradition, Transition, Justice and Promise. We will begin with an overview of events that led up to this emphasis and the worldwide decade for which it is named. The story is too vast for any one book to contain it all, but we hope this one offers enough to generate serious encounters between men and women about the faith we have inherited.

As we have been overwhelmingly reminded while working on this theme, a book about the churches in solidarity with women is about an idea whose time has come, an idea that is "breaking out all over." It is about the church's realization, one more time, that God is doing a new thing in Jesus, the Christ, and that this new thing has to do with breaking down the walls that separate. When this book focuses on past and present patterns of believing and relating, it deals with what has separated women and men. But in the process, we have found, the other barriers by which human creatures separate themselves from one another quickly surface as well. The promise of the very act of focusing on a specific kind of separation is that women and men together are beginning to find a new way.

This book can be a tool for beginning that new way. It can be the basis for joint discussions, studies, workshops involving both men and women. It is hoped that in local churches across this continent men will be willing to join women to talk about the nature of the church and about why the church continues to marginalize women in its life and mission.

Aruna Gnanadason of India, director of the World Council of Churches' Sub-Unit on Women in Church and Society, states the purpose of the decade from the woman's perspective in this way: "Our purpose is not to get small concessions from the church but to contribute our gifts so that the church can be transformed into a new and living community of women and men, playing a prophetic role in a world that so desperately needs a new vision."

*SC**

---

*Introductions and essays by the editor, Sarah Cunningham, are signed SC.

◇ **1** ◇

A Decade at Midpoint

The year 1993 marks the midpoint of the Ecumenical Decade of the Churches in Solidarity with Women. In summary, the goals of the decade are for women:

- to participate fully in church and community life;
- to share their perspectives and their commitments to justice, peace and the integrity of creation.
- to do theology and to share spirituality.

The decade invites churches to free themselves from teachings and practices that discriminate against women and that rob the church of women's gifts.

Solidarity! What Does It Mean?

It is very possible that we first heard the word "solidarity" associated with a social justice agenda, such as that of the labor movement or the church's "solidarity with the poor" in Latin America or the Solidarity movement in Poland in the 1980s, which drew working people and the church solidly together against an oppressive political system.

Within the church, "mutual interdependence" is the concept most often associated with the solidarity of women and men. When the church asks its members to be in solidarity with women, it is affirming its conviction that in partnership women and men rightly express the church's true nature. Women and men together make up the church and are called to its mission. And in terms of that mission, to be in solidarity with women means to stand as advocates with and for women everywhere, especially in settings where women are most exploited and oppressed.

The Ecumenical Decade of the Churches in Solidarity with Women was launched by the World Council of Churches at Eastertime in 1988 when it set in motion a ten-year process of paying

1

attention to those things that must change if women and men are to be equal partners in the mission of the church.

The decade involves Christian communions throughout the world, some of which date their history from the beginning of the Christian era. All have taken seriously the relationship between Christian unity and openness to women's leadership and authority.

The symbol for the decade is the bird of promise hovering over the ecumenical boat (itself a symbol of the church), with the sign of the New Woman in her beak and the future world in her womb. The symbol was the gift of Eva Saro, an artist from Geneva, "to all who would be in solidarity with women."

From the Beginning

Women have been a part of the church's story from the beginning. Mary, the mother of Jesus, said yes to God's gift of a child (Luke 1:38). Martha, sister of Lazarus, was among the first to announce her belief in Jesus as Messiah (John 11:27). Women were there at his crucifixion (see Matt. 27:55 ff.); Jesus appeared first after his resurrection to Mary Magdalene (Mark 16:9). "Certain women," including Jesus' mother, were with the disciples in the upper room "devoting themselves to prayer" following Jesus' ascension and preceding Pentecost (Acts 1:12ff).

Why have we been so blind to the New Testament evidence that women too were disciples of Jesus, were founders of churches in their houses (Acts 16:11–14, 40), were deacons (1 Tim. 3:8ff.) and teachers and preachers (Acts 18:26)? The evidence is all there if we read the New Testament carefully.

Feminist scholar Elisabeth Schüssler Fiorenza reminds us that the New Testament canon "is a product of the patristic church, that is, a theological document of the 'historic winners.'" She is suggesting that what was eventually recorded and copied over the centuries as the collective memory of the early church was determined by the male leadership that did the recording and editing. To that extent, she believes, we must go "beyond the limits of the New Testament" in order to reconstruct what really went on in Jesus' lifetime and in the early days of the church regarding the role of women. This presupposes a sense of ownership in the church on the part of women. It suggests for Fiorenza that women should not settle for being "either victims of patriarchal religion or collaborators with it."[1]

Despite the probable suppression of evidence of women's presence in the early church, there is enough evidence remaining in the historical record to make it quite clear that Jesus was proclaiming a new understanding of relationships between men and women. As one of the earliest confessions of the church proclaims: there is no longer Jew or Greek, slave or free, male and female, but all are one in Christ Jesus (Gal. 3:28).

A World Church Movement

Since it is beyond this book's scope to examine the church's two-thousand-year history of repression of women's leadership, we must simply acknowledge it as fact and focus now on the events of this century that have led us to launch the Ecumenical Decade of the Churches in Solidarity with Women.

Certainly the effort to persuade the churches to confront the issue of woman's place in the church has been on the World Council of Churches' agenda since its formation in 1948, and even before that, in world gatherings such as the 1927 Faith and Order meeting of several hundred church representatives in Lausanne, Switzerland.

By 1949, the Central Committee of the WCC had established the Commission on the Life and Work of Women in the Church, chaired by Sarah Chakko of the Syrian Orthodox Church of India. Commenting a year later on the need for such a commission, Willem Visser 't Hooft, the first general secretary of the WCC, said, "We are taking up this work when there is a specific crisis in the relationship of men and women, and in the world of women themselves.... Have Christians anything specific to say in this situation? The churches

---

1. Elisabeth Schüssler Fiorenza, *In Memory of Her: A Feminist Theological Reconstruction of Christian Origins* (New York: Crossroad, 1985), Introduction.

LAST AT THE CROSS

The women...remained with Jesus as he died. Their loyalty and bravery are obvious, and are clearly meant to contrast with the actions of Judas, the disciple who betrayed Christ, and with those of Peter, the disciple who denied him.

Yet Peter, despite his denial, is one of the great saints of the church, celebrated as the founder of the line of priests who made Christianity possible. Joseph of Arimathea, who procured the body for burial, is remembered in story and song. But the women at the cross are easily overlooked. Indeed, only a few weeks ago I read an otherwise wonderful sermon, a sermon so good that it was published as part of a distinguished sermon series, in which the writer declared that Jesus had died all alone, because all of his disciples had left him. Yesterday morning a speaker at a church meeting declared that when Jesus died, "only eleven men" were left in the world to do his work. "And," he then added, "a handful of others." Clearly, these statements reflect a common failing, a tendency to see only the people who one thinks are important in a scene or an event, and to forget or overlook the others. But there were others to carry on Jesus' work; some of them were women and some of those women were with him at the cross....

Two days later, it was women alone who came to the tomb to anoint the body, and discovered the empty tomb...being last at the cross and first at the tomb, ministering to the body of Christ.

Now, two thousand years later, the phrase "the body of Christ" has taken on a larger meaning. It's like the phrase "the body politic," and it refers at least on one level to the sense of shared beliefs that make us a religious community and to the covenant that binds us together. But it is important to remember that before there was a community called the Body of Christ there was a literal, flesh-and-blood body of Christ, to which women ministered. Yet somehow, as we have preached Christianity, we have let these women and their story be overlooked.

— Nanette M. Roberts, "Last at the Cross," *Spinning a Sacred Yarn: Women Speak from the Pulpit* (New York: Pilgrim Press, 1982), 172–74 have not yet said anything helpful on the subject, either separately or together. The time has come to say something extremely clear.... We must spend considerable time on laying the foundations now."[2]

By 1954, the WCC had established its Office of Cooperation of Men and Women in Church and Society, and Madeleine Barot of France was its secretary. The title of the office itself was an indication of progress. The Council now recognized that the solution was not simply a separate office to take care of "women's work"; rather, the real issue was how to bring about genuine cooperation and partnership between men and women in the church, and in the world as well.[3]

In 1975 the entire Fifth Assembly of the WCC, meeting in Nairobi, included concerns of women as a part of the observance of the United Nations–sponsored International Women's Year. This followed a 1974 special session held in Berlin. This session on "Sexism in the 70s" was staffed by Brigalia Bam of South Africa. By the summer of 1981, after a significant conference on the Community of Women and Men in the Church, in Sheffield, England,[4] the WCC's Central Committee, meeting in Dresden, affirmed women as "full participants in its life and work." What to most women seemed an obvious necessity "set the Committee apart from many of its member churches, and indeed over and against some of them," according to Mercy Oduyoye of Nigeria, formerly a deputy secretary of the WCC. Oduyoye's book, *Who Will Roll the Stone Away?* describes the intent of the 1988–1998 Ecumenical Decade of the Churches in Solidarity with Women.[5]

Meantime, in North America

By the late 1960s, large numbers of U.S. and Canadian church women were reading two widely available paperback books, books

2. Susannah Herzel, *A Voice for Women* (Geneva: World Council of Churches, 1981), 12.

3. In the 1970s, the office became the WCC Sub-unit on Women in Church and Society; while women's partnership with men was more and more affirmed by the churches, it was recognized that at this stage of the journey toward equality, issues of direct concern to and about women were too easily overlooked unless attention was specifically focused on them — and overwhelmingly, this attention first came from women themselves. For a discussion of similar searches for women's most effective "place" in the structures of denominations, see pages 105–108 below.

4. Constance F. Parvey, ed., *The Community of Women and Men in the Church, The Sheffield Report* (Philadelphia: Fortress Press, 1983).

5. Mercy Oduyoye, *Who Will Roll the Stone Away?* WCC Risk book (Geneva: World Council of Churches, 1990).

of both recognition and liberation: Betty Friedan's *The Feminine Mystique* and Simone de Beauvoir's *The Second Sex*.[6] In fact, during the late 1960s and early 1970s these two books were appearing on national reading lists of denominational women's groups. At last women had easy access to books that were describing a reality they knew by experience. The women's liberation movement had begun.

Actually, the movement was a revival of the nineteenth- and early twentieth-century women's movement and an extension of the ferment that had been building quietly since World War II, gaining visibility during the next two decades, and, by the 1970s, bursting upon the horizon in all its profusion of color, commitment, anger and boisterousness. Those were liberation days, and the women's movement went hand in hand with the black liberation movement as women saw many similarities between the oppression of African Americans and the oppression of women. Later, black women were to make significant distinctions between what was coined, by poet and novelist Alice Walker, as the womanist movement and what had come generally to be known as the feminist movement.

In the United States, these women's movements produced radically new kinds of publications and other media, spawned the National Organization of Women (NOW), resulting in political statements and candidates; called for political, social and religious reform; and resurrected the Equal Rights Amendment (first proposed in the 1920s). They succeeded in getting the amendment passed by Congress in the early 1970s only to see it eventually defeated in the next decade by lack of support from the fifty states.

In the meantime, however, the movement was gaining momentum everywhere. The national dynamics in each country were different, but the issues were basically the same. We need only look back briefly to realize why such a movement was necessary, indeed was inevitable.

As is always true in times of national or world crises, during World War II women were summoned from their homes and circumscribed environments to help win the war. They worked in munitions plants and army and navy supply factories. They ran hospitals, food centers, government offices and clothing industries, providing all the services necessary for civilian life. And many volunteered to serve in the military forces along with the men.

---

6. Betty Friedan, *The Feminine Mystique* (New York: W. W. Norton & Company, 1963); Simone de Beauvoir, *The Second Sex* (New York: Alfred A. Knopf, 1953).

After the war, they were expected to disappear again into their private worlds, but instead, following the baby boom and a few years of homemaking, women were ready again for a wider world and demanded change: change in opportunities for education, for work, for health care, for involvement in decisions about their own lives and in all aspects of the life of their community. They were ready for leadership in every institution. Women were claiming their total humanity and their place in the world. They were saying, yes, woman's place is in the home, and the world is our home.

A New Solidarity Emerges

The first ecumenical expression of a new consciousness and solidarity among U.S. church women came in 1969 when women delegates to the General Assembly of the National Council of Churches of Christ, meeting in Detroit, presented a statement of grievances to the Assembly.

The group defined itself as an informal caucus made up of some of the women voting delegates to the assembly plus others. Excerpts from their statement follow:

> We begin our statement with an affirmation of support for the movement to liberate women in the United States....
>
> Many who are seated here may be unaware of the unrest that is growing among thinking women, an unrest that is finding expression in formally organized fashion across the country.... The women of this country are gathering themselves into a sweat of civil revolt, and the general population seems totally unaware of what is happening; or indeed that anything is happening; or that there is a legitimate need behind what is happening.

The statement went on to point out that women in the U.S. "make 60 cents for every $1 a man makes" (a fact that has not changed noticeably since 1969). It noted women's lack of voice in government, private enterprise and church. The statement was also cognizant that:

> When we look back into history, we know as well as blacks know that "we've been here before." We've experienced change up to a certain point, only to fall back. We are now serving notice, and if we do not, others will, that we will finish the job this time.

And the women's vision was for the whole, ecumenical church:

> We want you to recognize that when we talk about women's
> liberation in the life of the church we are thinking about what
> is going on in the Roman Catholic Church as well as in Prot-
> estant and Orthodox churches, that we are talking about what
> is happening to women in the black churches as well as in the
> predominantly white churches.

After pointing out that "women are rising," the statement addressed the "male-dominated and male-oriented churches." The
church "has shown no propensity to transcend culture, as regards
the status of women, although it knows it ought." Citing statistics
that indicated that only 6 percent of the NCC's General Board were
women and that thirteen denominations were not represented by
any women delegates, it addressed the lack of female leadership in
all the denominations represented in the Council. It also pointed out
inequities in both hiring and salary levels among church staff both
denominationally and ecumenically.

The statement was forthright in expressing women's insistence on
justice for their half of the human race and their determination to
call the church to accountability in this task. The document closed
by saying:

> In conclusion, we reiterate our support for the effort to liberate
> women. We announce to this Assembly that women are on the
> move, and, using a current phrase, we make the prediction that
> "the next great movement in history" will be ours.[7]

In the months and years that followed, women began to caucus in their separate denominations, pressing for inclusive language
in worship, for the elimination of sex-role stereotyping in church
school curriculum, for openness to women in seminaries, both as
students and faculty, for ordination of women in those denominations that had not already opened the doors to women and for fair
employment of women in all facets of ministry.

Denominational governing bodies were called upon to establish
official task forces and commissions to address women's concerns.
Studies began to emerge on the role of the minister's wife, on
women as Christian educators and missionaries and volunteers in
the church's mission and ministry. In fact, papers, magazines, books,

---

7. Included in Sarah Bentley Doely, *Women's Liberation and the Church* (New
York: Association Press, 1970), as Appendix A.

films, conferences and assemblies began to proliferate in all the denominations giving voice to women's concerns. It was as if all the pent-up feelings, emotions, sensitivities, all the repressed insights, research and wisdom accumulated by women for a lifetime had finally found voice.

Church Women as Consciousness Raisers

During the 1970s the traditional church women's organizations in both the United States and Canada recognized themselves as consciousness-raising groups for women and women's issues. At the ecumenical level, Church Women United took an active role in advocating women's rights and women's liberation.

By 1974, with a great deal of support from women's organizations in the U.S., Claire Randall was elected the first woman general secretary of the National Council of the Churches of Christ. In that year the NCCC also established its Commission on Women in Ministry. Prior to her election, Randall had been actively involved as a staff member of Church Women United in finding ways for women to become more aware of their second-class citizenship in the church and to advocate change.

The United Nations was persuaded to hold a world conference on women in Mexico City in 1975. North American church women were strongly influential in bringing this about and in supporting its goals. When the subsequent U.N. Decade for Women culminated in a grand celebration in Nairobi in 1985, church women were there in large numbers and with their own agenda. In many respects, the U.N. conference and the decade were controversial, but they raised the visibility of women worldwide and put their concerns for equality, development and peace firmly on the U.N. agenda — and on the churches' as well.

It was partly due to the momentum of the total women's movement that in 1978 women and men in the United States and Canada joined with women and men throughout the world in a series of regional conferences on the theme, "The Community of Women and Men in the Church."

Under the direction of Constance F. Parvey, a Lutheran pastor from the U.S. on the staff of the World Council of Churches, the program "enjoyed the most extensive grassroots participation of any such project in the history of the World Council of Churches."[8] It

---

8. Constance F. Parvey, ed., *The Community of Women and Men in the Church*, ix.

prepared the way for the Sheffield, England, consultation in 1981, which in turn led to the report to the WCC Central Committee and eventually to the launching of the Decade of the Churches in Solidarity with Women.

Protestant, Orthodox and Roman Catholic women were also reaching out to one another for dialogue through the sponsorship of the World Council of Churches and councils of churches at national and regional levels. The fact that more and more women of color were coming into church leadership positions added another kind of cultural exchange that was very important for women's liberation.

During the 1960s, Brigalia Bam of South Africa, as the WCC staff person for women's concerns, had been supported by U.S. women's groups in her meetings in the U.S. with Martin Luther King Jr. and Coretta King, and in Latin America with Dom Helder Camara and key Latin American women. Such exchanges helped link the women's movement and other liberation movements together in common commitment. Speaking of the significance of these meetings, Brigalia Bam observed:

> Many women in Europe had not had an opportunity to meet women from developing countries as equals. It's very hard for people who have always been on the giving side — whether the giving of money, education or the gospel — to be at the receiving end, receiving not tangible gifts, necessarily, but ideas and people's culture. It doesn't happen without difficulty; but I have seen it happen....It works the other way as well. I know how much it has taken for women of the Third World to grow in their understanding of the woman's struggle in the developed countries.
>
>   ...
>
> To understand that while you are preoccupied with, say, equality or abortion rights, your sister is anxiously awaiting her husband's release from South African police detention is consciously to accept responsibility for her freedom in her terms. What is important for you may be merely incidental for her by comparison...."[9]

Elsa Tamez, Latin American theologian and author, says it this way as she reminds us that in many places, especially among the impoverished, women are doubly exploited:

---

9. Susannah Herzel, *A Voice for Women*, 63–64.

The poor woman belongs to the oppressed class, and, on the other hand, she is discriminated against because of her sex.... The poverty-stricken woman, who struggles for her very life, feels discriminated against, kept at the margin of society because of her sex.... She feels that the male companions with whom she shares the same aspirations oppress her, often without realizing it.... Many centuries of bad habits characteristic of the male-dominant culture are deeply imbedded in men, and even in women, and need to be attacked at the roots.[10]

And so for the church, the women's movement — welcomed openheartedly by many, grudgingly acknowledged by many others — became one sign of a worldwide yearning for a new creation. Now, we can look back and see a lot of progress. We will never be the same again — men or women. Yet, when it comes to the systemic forces that rule women's lives, they are still, for the most part, in the control of the white male power structure.

As Susannah Herzel pointed out,

It is not just a matter of acknowledging the physical differences between men and women and saying, as most of us would, *"Vive la difference!"* It is rather recognizing that alongside this difference there have been different histories, different expectations, a different sense of identity and an association with the structures of power that have created a male-dominated order in almost all human society and certainly within the church, making it impossible for the church to foreshadow the truly human community.[11]

A Decade for All

Explaining the purpose of the Decade of the Churches in Solidarity with Women, Mary Ann Lundy, Presbyterian (USA), and Forrest C. Stith, United Methodist, co-chairpersons of the U.S. Committee of the Ecumenical Decade: Churches in Solidarity with Women, emphasize that this "is not a decade of women for women." Those who launched the decade were aware that church women have been networking — providing support and creative channels of growth and development for each other — for a long time. Furthermore, church women have been advocates for all women and children, and for all the oppressed everywhere for a long time. "The Ecumenical Decade

---

10. Elsa Tamez, "Women: A Latin American Approach," unpublished paper.
11. Susannah Herzel, *A Voice for Women*, 73.

is a time for men and women to work together," say Lundy and Stith, "to bring about changes in ecclesiastical and social structures that are obstacles to women's full personhood and participation."[12]

Affirming this purpose for Canadian churches as well, Vivian Harrower, executive director of the Women's Interchurch Council of Canada, says that Canadian churches are at different places in their involvement of women in positions of leadership and decision making, but this is a continuing concern during the decade. She also points out that "the marginalization of women in the churches is directly related to the marginalization of women in all of society" and that one of the purposes of the decade is to "help the church see that connection."

Canadian and U.S. churches must extend the ultimate aim of the decade, therefore, to include concern for women in poverty, women victims of family and institutional violence and violence against children, often related to the marginalization of women. In other words, the church is called to be in solidarity with women everywhere who are victims of oppressive systems.

But we are also reminded by those who envisioned this decade that it "will achieve its goals only if the knowledge, experience and commitment of women and men are developed into *new configurations at local levels....* As we tackle our issues of work and worship *in our own places* and as we struggle together for solutions to common problems, we will be forging solidarity with sisters and brothers across the continents."[13]

The decade, then, is addressed to the whole church — *men* as well as women. The task is to envision the church as a foretaste of, and an advocate for, a new humanity, characterized by love and justice for all.

SC

---

12. Melanie A. May, ed., *Women and Church: The Challenge of Ecumenical Solidarity in an Age of Alienation,* preface by Mary Ann Lundy and Forrest C. Stith (Grand Rapids: Wm. B. Eerdmans; New York: Friendship Press, 1991).

13. Ibid., italics added.

PART ONE

Rethinking the Tradition: The Bible and the Church

◇

Something has happened in the last twenty-five to thirty years to alter human consciousness, particularly in relation to our way of viewing the masculine and feminine nature of humanity. Philosophers, sociologists, theologians, biblical scholars, all are aware of this. Applying such an awareness to the church, it is now possible to question the patriarchal nature of the Christian tradition in a way that would have been unthinkable before.

The first essay that follows, by Phyllis Trible, reflects on both the rewards and the risks of reading the Bible through feminist eyes. Praising but also probing these ancient texts, she tells us why the Bible is still such an important and rich resource for her feminist journey. The next three essays are examples of how people of faith are rethinking the biblical and early church traditions in regard to their message about women and men created in God's image.

Randall Bailey and Jacquelyn Grant bring an African American perspective to their scholarship. Bailey reexamines stories from the Hebrew canon. Grant takes a fresh look at the meaning of Jesus for women in particular. Robin Scroggs reexamines traditional biblical scholarship in search of new perspectives on the writings of Paul. Their three distinct methods of reflecting on the Scriptures can be liberating for all of us.

Bailey's commentary is peppered with irony and humor as he challenges conventional interpretations of familiar stories. Grant has described her own style as "polemic." She is forceful in presenting her case, illustrating it by referring to a range of both classical and recent sources. Scroggs allows the Scriptures to illuminate new truths in their own terms and in light of new interpretations by leading scholars.

We have invited people to write for us who are willing to risk asking new questions of our biblical literature. To be African American in this culture, or to be a woman, or to be both is to bring to the Bible a set of questions different from those of the prevailing culture. To be a seminary professor open to the questions of women and other persons who have been oppressed by the prevailing culture demands a kind of inquiry into the meaning of Scriptures that many be new to many readers.

But if you can allow yourselves to experience the work of the four persons who here offer a "Rethinking of the Biblical Tradition," you may discover that you have become much more curious and much more excited yourself about the revelations that await you. All four writers remind us that the Bible is our sacred literature, but also that it is story and poetry, prophecy and revelation more than it is doctrine or creed. Therefore, we must examine it anew in every age asking of it "the word of life" for *our* time.

SC

2

The Pilgrim Bible

PHYLLIS TRIBLE

In the following excerpt from a lengthier address, biblical scholar Phyllis Trible writes of "redeeming" the ancient traditions from the confines of patriarchy.   *SC*

◊

THE STORY BEGAN in the early 1970s. Listening to the animated discussions about feminism, I did not have to be converted but realized it was bone of my bones and flesh of my flesh. At the same time, I also understood that Scripture nourished my life; that the Bible I grew up with in Sunday School, where sword[1] drills were routine and memory verses mandatory, continued to feed me. To be sure, I had learned in college and graduate school that Scripture differs from what the church taught about it, but never did critical scholarship diminish my love for it. There is power in the document, and it need not work adversely for women or for men. This I knew and this I know, no matter how much others say it is not so.

But there was the rub. A feminist who loves the Bible.... That predicament has spurred rewarding study.... The Bible was born and

---

Phyllis Trible is Baldwin Professor of Sacred Literature at Union Theological Seminary. From an address delivered in October 1987 on "What Women Theologians Are Saying," excerpted as "The Pilgrim Bible on a Feminist Journey," *Auburn News* (Auburn Theological Seminary, New York), Spring 1988.

1. At one time, in many churches, sword drills were very popular among children and youth, and perhaps still are. They were drills in finding or reciting from memory biblical verses. Perhaps the name came from the idea that the "sword of the spirit...is the word of God" (Eph. 6:17b). In this case "the word" meant the Bible. —Ed.

bred in a land of patriarchy; it abounds in male imagery and language. For centuries interpreters have exploited this androcentrism to articulate theology, to define the church, synagogue and academy, and to instruct human beings, female and male, in who they are, what roles they should play, and how they should behave. So harmonious has seemed this association of Scripture with sexism, of faith with culture, that few have ever questioned it. Understandably, then, when feminism turns attention to the Bible, it first of all names patriarchy. To name means more than affixing a label. To name is to analyze and also to indict. The Bible promotes the sin of patriarchy.

Evidence abounds for the subordination, inferiority and abuse of women. One has no difficulty in making the case against the Bible....Yet the recognition has led to different conclusions. Some people denounce Scripture as hopelessly misogynous, a woman-hating document with no health in it....Other individuals consider the Bible to be an historical document devoid of continuing authority and hence worthy of dismissal. The "who cares?" question often comes at this point. In contrast, others despair about the ever-present male power that the Bible and its commentators promote. And still others, unwilling to let the case against women be the determining word, insist that text and interpreter provide a more excellent way. Thereby they seek to redeem the past (an ancient document) and the present (its continuing use) from the confines of patriarchy.

This last approach is my niche. Combining scriptural critique and feminist perspective shapes a hermeneutic that makes a difference. It begins with suspicion and becomes subversion. The goal is healing, wholeness, joy and well-being....

Reinterpretation characterizes this hermeneutic...but does not make the Bible say anything one wants. Between a single meaning and unlimited meanings lies a spectrum of legitimate readings. Some assert themselves forcibly; others have to be teased out....

The Bible wanders through history, engaging in new settings and ever refusing to be locked in the box of the past. Every generation and group who meet the test hold perspectives not adopted by others, pose questions not asked by others and discuss issues not raised by others. One group seeks what another did not. Each sees in part, not in whole. So this pilgrim book has maintained a lively dialogue with generations of readers....The feminist reinterpretations respect the historical, sociological, political and existential journeys of Scripture....

There are miles to go in exegesis and appropriation. At times, travel is difficult and dangerous. Like Jeremiah, I sense that enemies are around to reproach and denounce. At other times, the journey is fun. I know the joy of discovery, wholeness and well-being. Where will it all end? In my eschatological vision we move toward a theology of gender redemption, the healing of female and male. Upon arrival, the pilgrim Bible on a feminist journey will have returned us to creation in the image of God, a consummation devoutly to be sought.

3

Doing the Wrong Thing: Male-Female Relationships in the Hebrew Canon

RANDALL C. BAILEY

OFTEN WHEN WE THINK OF THE BIBLE, we think of a book with guidelines for our everyday living. Similarly, when we think of the famous figures in the stories of the Bible, we think of people who are held up as paragons of virtue.

The argument of this chapter, as you might suspect from the title, is that in regard to male-female relationships, the Bible may not be the place to look for positive role models. Were contemporary psychologists and social workers to use some of the stories in the Bible as intake data, they would have to give some painful diagnoses. The classical definition of a "dysfunctional family" could well be illustrated by stories from the Bible.

As we will see, Adam and Eve, Abraham and Sarah, Hagar, Ruth and Boaz, and the ideal wife of Proverbs 31 and her husband do not present us with viable, positive models for our own male-female relationships. Jealousy, mistrust, misuse and exploitation often undergird these relationships. Perhaps such stories provide us with a model more of what *not* to do in our relationships than of what to do. In fact, this might have been one intention of the ancient writers of these passages in the first place.

Randall C. Bailey is associate professor of Old Testament and Hebrew at the Interdenominational Theological Center, Atlanta, Georgia.

The method used in analyzing the Bible passages under investigation here is to pay close attention to the wording of the stories themselves, especially as they reveal values and motives of either the characters or the writers. In other words, what values must be operating in order for the actions or inactions of these characters to make sense to the reader? Attention is also paid to omissions in the stories. What things are not said? What options for action are not made available to the characters? Are these omissions due to the writer's narrative technique or to the social situation in which these characters are operating? The question is then raised, what does this story say to us today in terms of our own male-female relationships?

You may find it helpful to read the biblical passages noted for each section first, thus becoming familiar with the story line. As references are made to certain parts of the passage, you might want to reread those passages, as a way of checking the interpretation.

The Curse from the Garden
Genesis 3:1–19

The story of the Garden of Eden has wrongly been used over the centuries to argue that women are the root of all evil. Thanks to the work of feminist scholars such as Phyllis Trible, we have been able to rethink the story and see new and different meanings in the text.[1] Such insights come from paying close attention to the wording and nuances of the biblical narrative, which give us clues about the possible intention of the writer.

We are told at the beginning that "the serpent was more crafty than any other wild animal that the LORD God had made" (v. 1). The serpent enters into dialogue with the woman regarding God's commands about eating from the fruit in the garden. The woman answers him by saying, "We may eat of the fruit of the trees in the garden; but God said, 'You shall not eat of the fruit of the tree that is in the middle of the garden, nor shall you touch it, or you shall die'" (vv. 2–3).

This answer is most interesting for three reasons. First, the prohibition on eating the fruit (2:16–17) is given to the man, prior to the creation of the woman. In her response to the serpent, however, she uses the word "we," which shows that she understands that the law relates not only to men but also to women. She has included herself and claims all rights, duties and privileges of human exis-

---

1. See Trible, *God and the Rhetoric of Sexuality* (Philadelphia: Fortress, 1978).

tence. Though she was not present and therefore not addressed at that time, she realizes that she is also bound by the law and she is also aware of its requirements.

Second, a reason akin to the first, we see that the woman is presented as the one negotiating for the family. She is the spokesperson for herself and her husband. She is the negotiator, a valued position.

Third, the woman functions as a theologian as she reinterprets the law. If we look closely at the prohibition in Genesis 2:17, we see that all that is prohibited is the eating of the fruit. In Genesis 3:3 the woman responds by saying that not only are they not to eat of the fruit, they are not to "touch it." This added prohibition is based on a principle, no doubt well known to the narrator, of "placing a fence around the law," that is, using minor prohibitions to provide safeguards that would make violation of the main prohibition less likely. In other words, if one is forbidden even to touch the fruit, one is less likely to eat it. (We see another example of "placing a fence around the law" in Genesis 26:11, where Abimelech, king of Gerar, tries to put to rest Isaac's fears of having his wife taken from him and of being killed by saying, "Whoever touches this man or his wife shall be put to death.")

Thus, the narrator presents the woman not only as the family negotiator but also as a theologian, operating within the common bounds of theological discourse of the day.

As the story continues, the serpent counteracts the prohibition by arguing that rather than causing death, eating from the tree will make one knowledgeable (your eyes will be opened, v. 5a) and immortal (you will be like God, 5b). The woman did not just take the serpent at its word. Rather, the narrator tells us, she "saw that the tree was good for food, and that it was a delight to the eyes, and that the tree was desired to make one wise" (v. 6). In other words, she did her own assessment of the situation and arrived at a reasoned conclusion before she ate.

Contrary to the depiction of the woman as theologian and rational thinker who uses her intellectual powers before acting, the man is presented as totally uninvolved in such activity. We are told that "she also gave some to her husband, *who was with her,* and he ate" (v. 6b). In using such words the narrator tells the reader that the husband was present during the dialogue and negotiations. The narrator also tells us, by omission, that not only did the husband not object to the woman's actions, but that unlike the woman, who used her intellectual powers prior to acting, the man impulsively acted: "he ate." In other words, not only does he not speak in this part of the story, but there is no detailing of his intellectual activity prior to his action, only a description of his action. The contrast between the narrator's depictions of the woman and the man is stark in building up her intellect as opposed to his.

As the story goes on, the man and the woman act in concert. Their eyes are opened and they make fig-leaf coverings, and they hear "the sound of the LORD God" and hide themselves (vv. 7–8). When the LORD God opens the dialogue with them, however, the man speaks. Interestingly, though, in responding to God's question, "Where are you?" (v. 9), the man blurts out, "I heard the sound of you in the garden, and I was afraid, because I was naked; and I hid myself" (v. 10). Now God didn't ask for all that. Nor is the man's answer in terms of the two of them; rather, it is focused totally on himself (the word "I" appears four times in this speech). At the same time, his response to the simple question spills the beans.

When God asks the man how he knows he is naked and whether he has eaten from the tree, the man blames the woman. As he does so, he blames God, ("the woman *whom you gave* to be with me") and shuns responsibility, ("she gave me fruit," v. 12). "Don't blame me, she made me do it, and it's your fault for giving her to me in the first place," so to speak. Only then does he admit his action. Similarly, the woman doesn't accept full responsibility for her actions, for she says, "The serpent tricked me" (v. 13). The verbs by which the two lay blame again bespeak the narrator's bias. The man claims that the woman "gave," but she claims that the serpent "tricked," which again connotes intellectual activity.

As a result of these activities, both of these people are cursed by God. The curse for the woman is that she will suffer pain in giving birth to children and be subject to this man (v. 16). The curse for the man is that he will be alienated from the earth and from work (vv. 17–19).

This story gives us several points regarding male-female relationships. First is that for a woman to be subject to a man is a curse. Subjection is not the ideal situation envisioned by God. Rather, it is a negative relationship presented as a consequence of previous actions. The ideal situation is one of men and women working in concert.

Second, the story, as depicted in our analysis of the dynamics of the narrative, presents a situation in which an intellectually astute and sophisticated woman is made subject to a weak and impulsive male, who will not even accept responsibility for his actions. Such a relationship (and we all are aware of several of this type) is truly a curse. In a society that overvalues male input and oppresses women, we often see women downplaying their own skills and abilities in order to make their mate "shine." Not only do such relationships become unfulfilling, but they also take on the full weight of cursed existence. Thus, we would not recommend such a story as a paradigm for healthy male-female relationship. Rather, living according to the curse could be termed "doing the wrong thing!"

Finally, we began by arguing that this passage has been misused to label women as the temptresses and purveyors of evil. We would hope that our analysis would not lead to mislabeling men as ineffective, emotive idiots on the order of the man in this story. Let us not copy misguided and oppressive models of interpretation as we struggle for fresh insights into the text.

Jeopardizing the Matriarch
Genesis 12:10–20; 20:1–18; 26:6–11

Three stories found in Genesis depict the founding parents of ancient Israel in a compromising situation. In each of these stories a husband and wife are entering a foreign land. The husband speculates that his life will be jeopardized if the foreigners think that the woman with him is his wife. This fear is predicated on his assumption that these foreigners are deviant individuals who would kill a man in order to marry his wife. The solution proposed by the man is that his wife should pretend to be his sister, which she does in each instance. As a result of this ruse, in the first two situations, Sarai/Sarah ends up in the household first of Pharaoh (chap. 12) and then of Abimelech (chap. 20). In the third situation, the trick is discovered before Rebekah ends up in the household of Abimelech (chap. 26). Finally, the deceptions are discovered, the matriarchs are returned and the patriarchs are rewarded with property in the case of Abraham and Sarah, and with protective legislation in the case of Isaac and Rebekah.

Scholars have long argued that the two stories in Genesis 12 and 20 are parallel stories from the hands of two different writers, one in the tenth century B.C.E.,[2] and the other in the eighth century B.C.E. They have also maintained that the purpose of the second story was to eliminate the ethical problems posed by the writer of the first story. Let us, therefore, take a look at what these problems were.

First is the fact that the patriarch speculates erroneously that the

---

2. B.C.E, Before Common Era, and C.E., Common Era, are terms that replace B.C. and A.D., which have a direct Christian reference.

foreigners would kill a man to gain his wife. (Interestingly, in all three stories, the foreigners do live by the patriarchal customs of the day, including the right of a man to have more than one wife, but it could be argued that in some respects, they appear to be more upright and ethical than our ancestors in the faith.) Second is the lie told by the patriarch about his relationship with the matriarch. Third is her complicity in the scheme and the resulting jeopardy to her own well-being. Fourth is the question of what happened in the household of the foreign king. Fifth is the patriarch's profit as a result of the trickery.

In the second story, only two of these five ethical problems are addressed, the second and fourth. The writer of this story tells us that, when confronted by Abimelech about the lie and its possible consequences (20:10), Abraham responds with the argument that he really didn't lie, since Sarah is his half-sister (v. 12). Similarly, though the first story says that Pharaoh took Sarai as his wife (12:19), implying sexual relations, the writer of the second story pointedly states that he "had not approached her" (20:4).

The fact that the other three ethical problems already mentioned — unjustifiably demeaning the foreigner, jeopardizing the matriarch and profiting from trickery — remain constant in all three narratives, suggests that these behaviors were not unheard of in that time. But are they helpful paradigms for modeling our female-male relationships? I would think not.

On the one hand, the premise of each of the stories is the patriarch's unrealized fantasy that his life is in jeopardy. His solution then is to place his spouse in jeopardy in order to save his own life. Such solutions do not help establish trust in a relationship, to say the least.

On the other hand, in each story the matriarch goes along with this situation. We are not ever told how willing she was. In fact, the narrator pays little attention to her, giving her no words to speak in the story and giving us no indication of her feelings. Such lack of attention gives the impression that her feelings about the plan are of no consequence. Is this, one wonders, how the writer wants us to view her role in the relationship: as a piece of property that is expendable? All we know is that she does go along with the "program." In this way she becomes either a co-conspirator with her husband or a contributor to her own victimization. We don't have the details necessary to know which. What we do have, however, is the indication that both options are examples of doing the wrong thing.

As the stories in Genesis 12 and 20 end, the patriarch is the one to profit by the trickery. While Sarai/Sarah may have cooperated because of her husband, she was the one who had to pay the price. Clearly, this model for relationship is not viable. Thus, while most scholars label this story series with the literary motif, "she's my sister," that title is too benign. Given what happens in these stories and in these relationships, it seems more appropriate to label them, "the jeopardizing of the matriarch." In so doing, we are less likely to miss the negative message and example found here.

Exploitation and Lateral Violence
Genesis 16:1–16

The problem began when God promised Abram that his descendants would be as numerous as the stars (Gen. 15:4–5). This sounded good, but by chapter 16, years later, there was still no heir on the way. It was frustrating to live under a promise that was not fulfilled. It was even more frustrating to live under a promise from God that God was thwarting. As Sarai told Abram, "the LORD has prevented me from bearing children."

What do we do when God is the source of the problem, or so it seems to us? On the one hand, God has promised an heir. On the other, Sarai is barren. Not having children was a mark of shame in those days, since a woman's worth was based upon the children she could produce. We see this from the number of barren women stories in the Bible, such as Rachel (Gen. 30), Samson's mother (Judges 13), Hannah (1 Sam. 1) and the Shunammite woman (2 Kings 4), to name a few.

The problem was compounded when Sarai bought into such a definition of selfhood. As she says to Abram, "Go in to my slave girl; it may be that I shall obtain children by her." In order to achieve her desired status of childbearer, she was willing to share her husband with another woman. At the same time, Sarai was also willing to exploit this other woman by wishing to claim for herself the children the other woman bore. What we will do in order to live up to oppressive claims of the societies in which we live! We have to understand Sarai as a victim of such an order, one who has accepted the terms of her oppression.

As the writer tells us, Abram willingly went along with the program. As with Adam in Genesis 3, no protest is lodged by this man to the suggestion that he enter into relationship with Hagar for Sarai's benefit. The writer tells us he listened to her and did as she said.

What about Hagar? What about her feelings in the situation? Thanks to the work of such scholars as Renita Weems, Katie Cannon and Elsa Tamez, we have been sensitized to reconsider her part in the narrative. The narrator gives Hagar nothing to say in this part of the story. Rather, we see her acted upon by Sarai and Abram.

When Hagar is depicted, we see that she has partially accomplished Sarai's objective by getting pregnant. The narrator then tells us that she "looked with contempt on her mistress" (v. 4). The meaning of the phrase in the Hebrew wording of this verse is not entirely clear. Has Hagar also bought into the oppressive system's view of women, to the extent that she feels she is better than Sarai because she has conceived? Or is this phrase speaking to a sense of selfhood, which is not expected in servants? Is she being perceived as being "uppity"? Has she gotten out of her so-called place?

What complicates the matter is that Hagar is an Egyptian. This state of affairs, an Egyptian as a servant of nomadic people in Canaan, is most unusual, since in this historic period Egypt was the controlling force in the region. Having Hagar as a servant is almost like having a Getty or a Rockefeller as a domestic. Thus, what is meant by the phrase "looked with contempt" is most enigmatic.

As the story continues, Sarai and Abram get into a fight over Hagar. Abram tells Sarai to do with her as she pleases. What pleases Sarai is oppressing Hagar (vv. 5–6).

What is most sad about this story is the conflict that gets played out between Sarai and Hagar. In terms of the narrative, both are victims of a system that oppresses women. Similarly, both have bought into the system and its values. In so doing they have entered into conflict with each other instead of with the system. While they are battling it out, Abram is sitting back having it his way, exploiting both Sarai and Hagar. As far as he is concerned, he wins either way.

So often oppressed people enter into conflict with each other because it is easier than engaging the system and those in control. So often the system will support our oppressing others, as Abram does in supporting Sarai, as a means of keeping the oppression going. So often women of the privileged class, like Sarai, will side with the powers that be, rather than joining forces with their sisters from other oppressed groups. So often those who should be allies become enemies and, in so doing, buttress oppressive situations. Some women allow their relationships with men to dominate and dictate their relationships with other women to the detriment of all. Sarai and Hagar view each other as rivals for this man rather than victims of the system and of this man, who is benefiting from the system. As long as they view themselves within the framework of the system in which they live, they are trapped into this lateral violence.

The most troubling part of the story is the ending. Hagar decides that enough is enough and strikes out for her liberation. She meets the angel of the LORD. She is told that there is another generation on the way and she is sent back to Sarai "to submit to her" (v. 9). How could God do that? Why hasn't God taken the side of the oppressed in this situation? Perhaps the answer is in Hagar's being sent back to Sarai: that they have to work through and work out that relationship. Perhaps the answer is that the hope of the next generation for Hagar and Sarai will be found in the two of them working through this situation. Perhaps it is neither of these: perhaps God has sided with the oppressor.

Seduction for Economic Security?
Ruth 3:1–18

The book of Ruth is understood to have been written during the time of Ezra as a response to his efforts at reform in regard to intermarriage (Ezra 10:9–11). He decreed that all foreign wives should be sent home. The overall argument of the book of Ruth seems to be that Ruth was a Moabite, a foreigner, who was very pious and who accepted the God of Israel. Further, Ruth was depicted as the great-grandmother of King David (Ruth 4:17). Thus, the argument of the book is that, had the ancient Israelites in the time of the Judges gotten rid of foreign wives of Israelites, Ruth would not have been permitted to marry Boaz and we never would have gotten to David, who was viewed as the ideal king. Thus, the book of Ruth was a kind of polemic, an argument against Ezra's reform.

As the story goes, a Bethlehemite family moved to Moab during a famine. While there, the sons of this family married Moabite women. In time, both the father and the two sons died. Naomi, the mother and older widow, decided to return to her home in Judah. Ruth, one of the daughters-in-law, decides to go with her, while the other, Orpah, remains behind. Ruth gives her famous speech about adopting the God and people of Naomi (1:16–17). Such allegiance between two oppressed women is the exact opposite of what we saw between Sarai and Hagar.

Once in Bethlehem, Ruth becomes a scavenger in the fields of Boaz, a rich kinsman of Naomi (chap. 2). Boaz inquires as to who she is and takes a liking to Ruth. He then makes special arrangements for her to be taken care of in the gleaning fields (vv. 14–16).

The system of welfare in ancient Israel allowed strangers, orphans and widows to follow the reapers during harvest and pick up what was dropped (see Deut. 24:19–22). On the one hand this system allowed the poor to feed themselves. On the other, it locked them into a permanent underclass who were not landed or employed in such a way that they could independently take care of themselves.

When Ruth returned home after a day of gleaning, she informed Naomi of where she had been and what she had accomplished (vv. 19–21). Naomi evidently realized that they would not make it on such scavenging alone. Now another plan had to be put into operation (3:1). Thus she advised Ruth to wash and perfume herself, get dressed up and go down to the threshing floor where Boaz would be spending the night. She counseled Ruth to conceal herself until Boaz had had enough to eat and drink to feel content and ready for sleep. She was to watch to see where he went to lie down. Then Ruth was to go to him and do as Naomi had instructed: "Uncover his feet and lie down; and he will tell you what to do" (v. 4). In order to get the full impact of Naomi's plan, the reader needs to know that the word for feet was sometimes a euphemism for the genitals, and that to lie with another was a euphemism for sexual intercourse (see Deut. 22:22–24, 2 Sam. 11:8, 11). In essence, Naomi is telling Ruth to seduce Boaz. Ruth follows Naomi's instructions. Boaz complies (3:8–13).

What is interesting is that the narrator gives us these details but makes no evaluative comments about them. There are no clues that either woman is acting out of character or outside of the tradition. As the story continues, as a result of their experience that night, Boaz tricks the next of kin into relinquishing his claim on Ruth, so that he might marry her (chap. 4). The plan works.

While the modern Bible reader might be shocked at such goings-on in the Bible, we need to take a look at the dynamics of this situation to see what issues are raised for us. First we note that the situation in which Naomi and Ruth find themselves is financially untenable. They could continue trying to live off gleanings of the field, but to do so would not provide an economically secure life. The only viable economic security for a woman that the system offered was marriage. If Naomi and Ruth were to improve their lot in life, something else had to be done. They chose the seduction of Boaz.

This text raises for us the question of the options available to women, especially poor women, to move out of poverty. Is marriage the only way out? Does one have to engage in seduction as a means of achieving this? Is Boaz a victim or a willing co-conspirator in this scheme?

While Ruth is presented to us as the great-grandmother of David, thereby suggesting that this situation worked out for the best, we have to ask whether economic security is the best or even a good reason for marriage. Is Ruth the paradigm for solving such problems? What other options are available to women in her situation today?

What about the Boazes of today? How else can men respond to such situations today? What responsibility do they have to ensure that options are made available to women other than to enter into sexual relationships for economic security.?

These are hard questions, with no easy solution. What this book of the Bible does for us, however, is pose them and encourage us to struggle with them.

The "Type A" Mother
Proverbs 31:10–31

The passage in the closing chapter of the book of Proverbs is often held high as a paradigm for the woman of today. It is the passage most often used for "Women's Day" in our churches. It is also one of the most oppressive passages for women found in the Hebrew canon.

The passage begins by describing the worth of a *"capable woman"* for her husband (vv. 10–11). It continues on to detail the ways in which she is an economic asset to the family (vv. 12–22). She not only cooks and sews, she also grows her own food and works all day to serve her family. What is interesting is that most of the activities described, including farming (vv. 16–17) and marketing of her wares (v. 18), were generally male activities as well in that ancient society. Thus, the message is that her worth is evaluated not only in terms of ensuring the family's economic security, but also in the fact that she in reality acts like a man would act. This listing of her good qualities is extended in citing other such examples (vv. 24–27).

Both of these listings of her "good qualities" end by speaking of the activities of her husband (vv. 23 and 28b) and her children (v. 28a). The husband sits in the gates, where the elders of the city hold court, and pontificates. He and the children praise her and call her blessed (RSV) or happy (NRSV). She works and they benefit from her labors.

The poem closes with the instruction that she is to be praised for all that she does (vv. 29–31).

But is this a viable marriage? How often are women socialized into thinking that such behavior is required of them? How often are men socialized into thinking that such behavior is required of women? How many marriages or families require two salaries to survive economically, while at the same time assuming that the woman is not only to work outside the home but also to do all the work in the home? How many women end up not only holding down a nine-to-five, but also coming home to do the cooking and cleaning, and spending the weekend shuttling the children from culturally enriching activity to physically enriching activity? How many marriages do we see going down the tubes because of unrealistic and oppressive expectations on only one of the spouses? How often do we cripple each other by succumbing to the oppressive demands of society?

Perhaps we need to answer the question in verse 10, "A capable wife who can find?" by saying, "No one, we hope!"

Conclusion

There are other dimensions to all these stories, of course, and many excellent biblical scholars have addressed them. What we have been examining here are guidelines about how *not* to relate to each other as men and women. True, these comments have been short on the positive side of how to structure good relationships, but perhaps if we can begin to ask the critical questions, we will eventually find better answers.

◇ **4** ◇

Jesus and the Task
of Redemption

JACQUELYN GRANT

Across the centuries from the days of the earliest church, Christians have understood and honored Jesus Christ as their Redeemer, a concept itself drawn from the Hebrew canon. Yet Christians' pictures of what it means to have a redeemer are always shaped by human thinking and human culture. In this article, Jacquelyn Grant proposes that as human beings we, too, have our own task of redemption to do in relation to Jesus Christ. We need to redeem our understanding of who Jesus Christ is for us from those historical and cultural interpretations that have limited, even distorted, the person and work of Christ. And because women's experience has so seldom been considered when the church presents its understanding of Jesus Christ, women have a special responsibility to undertake this human task of redemption, bold though such a step may seem.

Thus, when the author speaks about "redeeming" or "reforming" or "liberating" Jesus Christ, she speaks about a shift she is convinced we need to make in our own understanding and interpretation of Jesus Christ.   *SC*

Jacquelyn Grant is associate professor of Systematic Theology at the Interdenominational Theological Center in Atlanta, Georgia. During 1991–92 she was the Willa Beatrice Player Visiting Professor of Humanities at Bennett College in Greensboro, North Carolina. She is the author of *White Women's Christ and Black Women's Jesus: Feminist Christology and Womanist Response* (Atlanta: Scholars Press, 1989).

◇

Christian theology tells us that Jesus Christ is the Redeemer. What sense then does it make to speak of redemption as a human task — and in particular as the task of women? That may sound presumptuous, yet the presumptuousness of the task does not negate its necessity.

To explore this phenomenal task as a part of women's work in the church, we shall explore four topics: (1) the historical imprisonment of Jesus Christ, (2) the reformation of Jesus Christ, (3) the liberation of Jesus Christ, (4) a womanist Jesus.

The Historical Imprisonment of the Redeemer

It is no accident that in the course of Christian history men have defined Jesus Christ so as to undergird their own privileged positions in the church and society. Evidence comes from the way that Jesus Christ is so often used to justify the subordination of women in the church. Before we look at how this is done, it is important to look at the context in which this kind of oppressive interpretation can emerge.

The social context in which Christianity as we know it developed and in which we now live can be labeled "patriarchy." Patriarchy is a reality defined in the male consciousness by which men dominate women. While men play primary roles, women are given secondary ones that, generally speaking, are subordinate. However, patriarchy "refers to more than a socially prescribed hierarchy of sex roles." It embraces all our assumptions about reality and behavior, about human nature and the cosmos "that have grown out of a culture in which men have dominated women."[1] That is to say, patriarchy is a way of looking at reality so that role assignments are not optional or arbitrarily given, but are prescribed by the rational and systematic structure of patriarchy itself. In this patriarchal system, men are central and women are marginal. In fact, patriarchy has been called a "conceptual trap" that ensnares its victims and keeps them in place through the constant reinforcements that come through the interlinking of all of the institutions of society that cooperate to keep the system in place. Living in the patriarchal system is like being in a room and being unable to imagine anything in the world outside

---

1. Sheila Collins, *A Different Heaven and Earth* (Valley Forge, Pa.: Judson Press, 1974), 51.

of that room.[2] It becomes difficult then for either men or women to imagine themselves moving outside their prescribed roles; when they do, they are treated as "exceptions."

Living within the parameters of the roles patriarchy assigns means that everyone adheres to the dualisms inherent in patriarchy. In other words, there is a double standard for men and women in our church and society. Men, it is believed, have a peculiar hold on intelligence because they make use of the mind and are rational, logical, deliberative and systematic. Women are associated with the body and are perceived to be irrational, illogical, intuitive and imaginative. The system also relies on hierarchy: the male role is considered superior, the female role is considered inferior. Consequently, men are independent and women are dependent.

Patriarchy is further reinforced through ordering the universe in a way to reflect the superior/inferior, independent/dependent relationship between men and women. This ordering has been described in religious terms as: God-Angels-Jesus-Men-Women-Children-Beasts-Plants-Earth-Evil.[3] The line of authority and power follows this hierarchical relationship. As Jesus has power and authority over men and women, so men have authority over women and children. In patriarchal structures, whether religious or nonreligious, women are generally secondary and subordinate to men.

What impact has the concept of patriarchy had on religious interpretation? More specifically, what has been its effect on the understanding of Jesus given to us through Christian history? One way to get at these questions is to examine the issue of leadership in the church. This issue is important in our task of "redeeming the redeemer," because historic arguments against women's liberation and for the oppression of women in the church have tended to take Christ as their starting point.

You have heard the argument in one or more variations. As Reginald Fuller summarizes the traditional points against ordaining women, these include:

The recorded call of disciples were all of men.... Jesus in his earthly life chose Twelve for a particular role — to be signs of the New Israel that would come into being with the advent of God's kingdom. The Twelve were men. If Jesus had intended

---

2. Elizabeth Gray, *Patriarchy as a Conceptual Trap* (Wellesley, Mass.: Roundtable Press, 1982), 17.

3. Collins, *A Different Heaven and Earth*, 66.

his church to have women ministers (leaders), it is argued, he would have included women among the Twelve.[4]

Some have been honest enough with themselves to say simply that women's leadership/ordination is not right or acceptable because we (the worshipers) are not used to it. This, in effect, is what David Stuart says:

Christ himself chose men to be apostles, the early church ordained men to be priests and consecrated men to be bishops. For generations the worshiper has heard the sounds of a male voice reading the prayers of consecration; for centuries the priest-confessor has been a man. Men were and continue to be the leaders, the initiators, the heads of households familial and ecclesiastical, and it would be psychologically confusing as well as historically disruptive to substitute women for that office. The long history of the Holy Catholic Church has been that of a male priesthood — this tradition is not hastily or lightly to be broken.[5]

Tradition is of primary importance here. The ethical issue of "rightness and wrongness" is not mentioned; justice is not considered; it seems that the "wasness and isness" — the simple historical past and present — is what counts.

As we see, the argument against women's leadership takes various historical, sociological and psychological forms. The argument that purports to be most theologically necessary draws on the doctrine of *Imago Dei*, the image of God. It is based on "representation" and "natural resemblance." In this argument, it is crucial that the one doing the representing — in this case, the ordained leader — be "in the image of," or by nature resemble, the one represented, Christ.[6] According to this reasoning, because Jesus was male, only males can represent Christ. The maleness is integral to the image. David Stuart asserts that "to change the sex of the priest alters the

---

4. Reginald Fuller, "Pro and Con: The Ordination of Women in the New Testament," in *Toward a New Theology of Ordination: Essays on the Ordination of Women,* ed. Marianna H. Micks and Charles P. Price (Somerville, Mass.: Greeno, Hadden and Co., 1976), 1.

5. The Rev. David R. Stuart (pseud.), "My Objections to Ordaining Women," in *The Ordination of Women: Pro and Con,* ed. Michael P. Hamilton and Nancy S. Montgomery (New York: Morehouse-Barlow Co., 1975), 47–48.

6. This argument is the one approved by Pope Paul VI and presented by Cardinal Franjo Seper to dismiss women's ordination and other related questions. See Cardinal Franjo Seper, "Vatican Declaration," *Origins, N.C. Documentary Service* (February 3, 1977): 6.

image of God."[7] This line of argument has been used in one way or another in many Protestant churches, as well as in other communions, to justify the continued exclusion of women from the ordained ministry and leadership of the church.

As maleness is dominant in patriarchal society in general, it is clear that in patriarchal religions maleness is likewise of utmost importance.

Lingering questions: If one could break free from the conceptual trap of patriarchy, would questions emerge to challenge some of the assumptions inherent in patriarchal interpretations of reality? For example, what about the unnamed women who surrounded Jesus? Isn't it conceivable that, consistent with patriarchal tendencies, the women were simply erased from history?

Some have suggested that even if Jesus had chosen women disciples, they would have been eliminated from the records anyway. I remember hearing noted church historian Cyril Richardson telling a story from early church literature in which a woman was put in a positive and active light. But, he said, a later editor, feeling that no woman could have said and done what was attributed to this one, changed the name of the person to that of a man. Women were active in the life of Jesus; however, the marginalization of women in our written texts could very well be a direct result of what happens in a patriarchal tradition.

Further, as church worshipers have been socialized to accept the male reality as normative, can't we be resocialized to become accustomed to the female reality? Asked another way, just as we have become accustomed to the male voice and leadership, isn't it conceivable that we could develop appreciation for the female voice and leadership?

But more importantly, have we noticed that even the power of God is compromised in patriarchal arguments? For example, the *Imago Dei* argument implies that God — the supernatural one — cannot transform the natural woman, only the natural man. Does this suggest that the woman is more powerful than even God?

When we examine the historical record, what we find is that Jesus has been imprisoned by the sin of patriarchy. The sin is the need to make Jesus and God in the image of man. Specifically, the sin is idolizing maleness. In spite of the power of this idolatry, women have not abandoned Jesus. Instead, women have attempted to redeem Jesus from the sin of patriarchy. Let us now

---

7. Stuart, "My Objections to Ordaining Women," 48.

turn to two ways in which women have attempted this redemptive process.

The Reformation of Jesus

Women have been working diligently to overcome the sin of patriarchy. They have been able to break away from the patriarchal trap by taking seriously women's experiences as the context for biblical interpretation. This has led to the rereading of biblical history, which has given evidence for new understandings of Jesus Christ, namely, (1) that Jesus was a nonconformist, (2) that Jesus was a model of wholeness, and (3) that Jesus was a feminist (one who affirmed women as persons created equally with men in the image of God).

Jesus the Nonconformist

In many respects, we are accustomed to preaching and teaching about the nonconformist nature of Jesus Christ. Generally, we associate his activities with his divinity and authority. So we accept interpretations of the gospels that elevate his nonconformity. Jesus went against religious law as he healed on the Sabbath; he defied natural law as he calmed the angry sea; he turned society's elitist customs on their heads when he dined with sinners and associated with outcasts; he redefined the laws of life and death as he raised the dead; he went beyond medical science as he healed the unhealable. We perceive all these unusual, unique and miraculous occurrences as reflections of the divinity and authority of Jesus Christ, the incarnation of God. In the same vein, we can perceive Jesus' unique actions toward women as representing God's unequivocal rejection of customs or laws that deny the equality of women and men.

In a society where laws and customs legislated the inferiority of women and denied them a role in the public world, Jesus dared to defy those unjust practices. He taught women (Luke 10:38–42), he touched women (Matt. 9:18), he defended women (John 8:1–11), he spoke to women (John 4:1–30), and he commissioned women (John 4:29, 20:17). The disciples did not understand these actions and often reminded Jesus of their inappropriateness. The disciples' view conformed to that of their world; the disciples and Jesus, observes Virginia Mollenkott, operated on different value systems. Consider for example, the passage in Matthew 18 where the male disciples squabble over "who is the greatest." Undergirding their understanding of "greatness" was a model of domination/submission. Jesus undercut the argument by totally relocating the place of greatness: "Whoever welcomes a little child like this in my name welcomes me" (Matt. 18:4–5 NIV). This reversal of the values of that day and today challenges the model of domination/submission and suggests that we need to acquire new ways of understanding human relationships.[8] Though there is no direct reference to women in this passage, the overturning of traditional oppressive ideas about relationships means that women's lives must be changed as well.

Rereading the New Testament through the eyes of women's experiences reveals that Jesus often violated the customs and cultural practices of his time. In a male-dominated society, Jesus' own actions distinguished him as a nonconformist. In fact, some have argued that he was a revolutionary when it came to his relationship with women. "He treated women as fully human, equal to men in every respect; no word of deprecation about women, as such, is ever found on his lips."[9]

Jesus the Model of Wholeness

Where the church fathers have chosen to accentuate the maleness of Jesus, I believe that women have tended to accentuate the humanness of Jesus. Some men also who are breaking out of the conceptual trap of patriarchy are reading the Scriptures anew. In trying to understand the psychology of the nonconformist Jesus, Leonard Swidler, among others, has pointed out that the Scriptures reveal that Jesus' actions were not limited to traditionally masculine behavior, but that he often displayed characteristics normally considered feminine as well.

Generally we expect men to be reasonable and cool and women to display feelings and emotions. In Luke 20:20–26 and 4:28–30, Jesus demonstrates reasonableness and coolness; but in Luke 7:11–15 and John 11:33–36, Jesus also expresses feelings and emotions. Firmness and aggressiveness are shown in Mark 8:33 and Luke 12:49 ("men's" traits), while gentleness and peacefulness ("women's" traits) are seen in Luke 13:34, Matthew 5:4, Luke 2:14 and 7:50. Men are generally associated with pride and self-confidence; so is Jesus in Matthew 21:8–10 and John 18:33–37 and 19:10. Women are associated with humility and reserve; so is Jesus in Luke 14:7–11 and Matthew 6:1–6. Like men, Jesus is the provider of security (food,

---

8. Virginia Mollenkott, *Women, Men and the Bible* (Nashville: Abingdon, 1977), 20.

9. Paul Jewett, *Man as Male and Female* (Grand Rapids, Mich.: Wm. B. Eerdmans Publishing Co., 1975), 94.

clothing and shelter) in John 6:6ff.,35 and Luke 12:22; like women, Jesus needs security in Matthew 15:34.[10]

Clearly, Jesus transformed traditional dichotomies that neatly divided men and women into separate categories and conveniently fed into patriarchal models of relationships. In patriarchal models, the traits of men are considered dominant, superior, more important; those of women are considered subordinate, inferior and less important. By manifesting both kinds of traits, Jesus violated what was expected of him as a man of his day. Swidler summarizes:

> In all the traditional categories of so-called feminine and masculine traits the image of Jesus that is projected is very strongly both.... The model of how to live an authentically human life that Jesus of the gospels presents is not one that fits the masculine stereotype, which automatically relegates the "soft," "feminine" traits to women as being beneath the male — nor indeed is it the opposite stereotype. Rather, it is an egalitarian model. Thus the same message that Jesus (and the gospel writers and their sources) taught in his words and dealings with women, namely, egalitarianism between women and men, was also taught by his own... lifestyle.[11]

Jesus the Feminist

Jesus' nonconformity and his unapologetic in-tuneness to both feminine and masculine worlds shows how Jesus differed from traditional, prescribed outlooks and attitudes. Given his relationships with and attitude toward women, it is reasonable to conclude that Jesus brought a different message, a message of dignity and liberation for women. We can only conclude, as Swidler did as early as twenty years ago, that "Jesus was a feminist."[12]

The Liberation of Jesus

But is it enough simply to "reform" our ways of perceiving Jesus through such new understandings? Some who have moved out of the patriarchal trap have been engaged in the process not only of reforming Jesus but also of liberating him. Two concepts that show

---

10. Leonard Swidler, *Biblical Affirmation of Women* (Philadelphia: Westminster Press, 1977), 282–90.

11. Ibid., 290.

12. Swidler, "Jesus was a Feminist," *Southeast Asia Journal of Theology* 12 (1971): 103. See also Rachel Wahlberg, *Jesus according to a Woman* (New York: Paulist Press, 1975). In Wahlberg's interpretations, women take more active positions as subjects.

possible ways of liberating Jesus Christ from the sins of patriarchy
are (1) Jesus Christ the representative and (2) Christ the sister.

Jesus Christ the Representative

Women's discussions of Jesus as "representative" take on a much
more liberating quality than the perceptions of Jesus within a patriarchal context. The traditional arguments against women's ordination
depend on Jesus as "representative" human in a very narrow, literal
way. Women, according to these interpretations, cannot meet the
"natural resemblance" requirement and therefore cannot represent
Christ. How, then, does or can Christ represent them?

Feminist interpretation of the representative solves this problem
by eliminating the need for such "natural resemblance." First, even
to speak of a "representative" accents the use of symbolism in our
religious language. This symbolism means that there is no direct or
precise correlation of the language with reality. So when feminists
speak of Jesus Christ as the representative, they are able to make
claims for inclusive participation in the new humanity. The maleness of Jesus, which has been used to oppress women, is not critical
for women. That maleness was part of what has been called the
"scandal of particularity": to be human, Christ had to come in some
concrete form, either male or female.

Some have attempted to deal with the dilemma of representation
by "looking for further incarnation in the form of a woman."[13] The
Shakers, for example, chose this route. Some have simply acknowledged that, given the social context of patriarchy, Jesus had to have
been a man; a woman could not have functioned in the society of
that time to effect salvation. These proponents argue that because
God knew the sin and weaknesses in the culture of the people, God
sent a man to do a woman's work. The "scandal of the maleness"
leads us to ask, "How is it possible for this male to be the bearer of
God's togetherness with women and men when he represents only
one half of the human race in this respect?"[14]

The challenge for us is to separate Christ's work from "maleness." For many, to redeem the redeemer is to connect Christ's work
with his being the new human; his maleness is incidental, his humanness is paramount. It is in the new humanity that we see the
representative work of Jesus taking effect.

---

13. Letty Russell, *Human Liberation in a Feminist Perspective — A Theology*
(Philadelphia: Westminster Press, 1974), 137.
14. Ibid., 138.

Christ the Sister

For some women, the conceptual trap has been totally eliminated. Not only are such women able to envision ways of reformulating Christian concepts, they are even able to reconceptualize, so as to project the previously unthinkable.

Some have gone back to the basics to ask the simple yet profound question, "Can a male savior save women?" Given what it means to be male and female in our church and larger society, the question challenges a basic assumption that has undergirded all of Christian thought, that is, that the male experience is universal; therefore, it suffices to represent all of reality. Yet human reality has been divided into dualisms, as discussed earlier. One manifestation of such dualism renders man as the protector and woman as the protected. Given the limitations placed upon women's lives, in order to maintain consistency with such a dualistic structure, one is forced to ask who/what is really being protected — women, or the "sacredness" of the privileged position of men? We have already seen that understandings of Jesus Christ, developed within the context of patriarchy, merely uphold patriarchal structures that oppress women. In what way is it meaningful to speak of a male savior "saving" women, if he has investments in those oppressive structures?

Jesus Christ must be liberated from captivity, so that we all can be liberated from the various forms of captivity that keep human beings enslaved. This liberation is redeeming; in fact it is mutual redemption. As we continue the process of liberating Jesus from patriarchal oppression, Jesus liberates us. Because the redemptive process itself still continues, we cannot limit the experience of the Christ to the historical Jesus, but we must remain open for redemption in contemporary times through new means. With this openness, we can even experience "Christ in the form of our sister."[15] The historical Jesus was a man, but men do not have a monopoly upon Christ. "Christ is not necessarily male, nor is the redeemed community only men, but new humanity, female and male."[16]

A Womanist Jesus

Jesus Christ has been a central figure in the lives of African American women. The Jesus of African American women has suffered a

---

15. Rosemary Ruether, *Sexism and God-Talk: Toward a Feminist Theology* (Boston: Beacon Press, 1983), 138.

16. Ibid.

double bondage. Not only has Jesus been held captive to the principles of patriarchy, but Jesus has also been imprisoned by the racism that has pervaded both our church and society. Jesus has been used to keep women in their proper place; likewise, he has been used to keep blacks meek, mild and docile, so that they will remain in their place as well. African American women heard twice the mandate, "Be subject..., for it is sanctioned by Jesus and ordained by God" (see 1 Pet. 2:18; 3:1.). In spite of this oppressive indoctrination, Jesus Christ has been a central figure in the lives of African American women. They have obviously experienced Jesus in ways different from what was intended by those who introduced them to the gospel. Three such experiences are (1) Jesus as co-sufferer, (2) Jesus as equalizer and (3) Jesus as liberator.

Jesus as Co-Sufferer

Chief among black people's experiences of Jesus is that he is a divine co-sufferer, who empowers them in situations of oppression. For Christian African American women of the past, Jesus was a center of reference. In spite of what was taught them, they were able to identify with Jesus, because they felt that Jesus identified with them in their sufferings. Just like them, Jesus suffered and was persecuted undeservedly. Jesus' sufferings culminated on the cross. African American women's cross experiences were constant in their daily lives — the abuses, physical and verbal, the acts of dehumanization, the pains, the sufferings. But because Jesus Christ was not a mere man, but God incarnate, they in fact connected with the Divine. This connection was maintained through their religious life — their prayer tradition and their song tradition. Their prayers were conversations with one who "walked dat hard walk up Calvary and ain't weary but tink about we all dat way."[17] The connection was also evidenced by the song tradition in which one could lament, "Nobody knows the trouble I see...but Jesus...."

Jesus as Equalizer

African American women had been told twice that their inferiority and inequality were a part of the nature of things. They, along with African American men, were taught that they were created to be the servant class for those in control. They were not to preach (in the case of women), and they were to acknowledge their place as a part of God's providence. But African American women experienced Jesus

---

17. Harold A. Carter, *The Prayer Tradition of Black People* (Valley Forge, Pa.: Judson Press, 1976), 49.

as a great equalizer, not only in the white world, but in the black world as well. And so they would argue that the crucifixion was for universal salvation, not just for male salvation or for white salvation. Because of this, Christ came and died, no less for the woman than for the man, no less for blacks than for whites.

> If the man may preach, because the Savior died for him, why not the woman? Seeing he died for her also. Is he not a whole savior, instead of a half one as those who hold it wrong for a woman to preach, would seem, to make it appear?[18]

Because Jesus Christ was for all, he in fact equalizes all and renders human oppressive limitations invalid.

Jesus the Liberator

Not only does Jesus equalize, but Jesus liberates. The liberation activities of Jesus empower African American women to be significantly engaged in the process of liberation. Sojourner Truth was empowered, so much so that when she was asked by a preacher if the source of her preaching was the Bible, she responded, "No honey, can't preach from de Bible — can't read a letter." Then she explained: "When I preaches, I has jest one text to preach from, an' I always preaches from this one. My text is, 'When I found Jesus!'" In this sermon Sojourner Truth talks about her life, from the time her parents were brought from Africa and sold, to the time that she met Jesus within the context of her struggles for dignity of black people and women.[19]

Summary

Both white women and black women have rethought their understandings of Jesus Christ. They have done so against the odds. For they both live in the context of a patriarchy that has enabled men to dominate theological thinking. Yet they have emerged to say that women's experiences must be taken seriously, and even if men refuse to do so, women must forge ahead nonetheless. Given our continuing patriarchal context, the task is a phenomenal one. Yet we must continue to talk about Jesus the Nonconformist, Jesus the Model of Wholeness, Jesus the Feminist, Jesus the Representative, Christ the

---

18. Jarena Lee, *Religious Experiences and Journal of Mrs. Jarena Lee* (Philadelphia, 1849), 15–16.

19. Olive Gilbert, *Sojourner Truth: Narrative and Book of Life*, 1850 and 1875; reprinted (Chicago: Johnson Publishing Company, Inc., 1970), 119.

Sister, Jesus the Co-Sufferer, Jesus the Equalizer, Jesus the Liberator and Jesus Christ as experienced in the lives of women of all races, colors and spiritualities, thus redeeming our understanding of Jesus Christ from the sins of patriarchy and racism. This is the phenomenal task of phenomenal women.

Yes, they will call us arrogant, presumptuous, audacious and boldacious. Yet we must be able to say:

> Now you understand
> Just why my head's not bowed,
> I don't shout or jump about
> Or have to talk real loud.
> When you see me passing
> It ought to make you proud.
> I say,
> It's in the click of my heels,
> The bend of my hair.
> The palm of my hand,
> The need for my care.
> 'Cause I'm a woman
> Phenomenally,
> Phenomenal woman,
> That's me.[20]

> — Maya Angelou

---

20. Maya Angelou, from the poem "Phenomenal Woman," in *And Still I Rise* (New York: Random House, 1978), 9–10.

Women and Men
in the Early Church

ROBIN SCROGGS

A QUIET REVOLUTION has occurred in New Testament scholarship, and this revolution is beginning to shake up the churches. Even twenty-five years ago church leaders and biblical scholars were of the opinion that the New Testament presented a unified view of the natural and divinely inspired dominance of male over female. Beginning in the early 1970s, however, we began to be aware that such a unified reading of New Testament texts was simplistic and did not do justice to what some texts said plainly and others implied.

In part the emerging tension about what the New Testament *really* said was dependent on one's judgment about what texts to begin with. Should we take as normative and typical the judgment in 1 Timothy 2:11–12: "Let a woman learn in silence with full submission. I permit no woman to teach or to have authority over a man"? Or perhaps Colossians 3:18: "Wives, be subject to your husbands, as is fitting in the Lord"? Traditionally these and similar texts were taken to be *the* New Testament word about the status and proper relationship of female to male.

Scholars, however, began to recognize that other texts presented a significantly greater acceptance of the equality of male and female in the emerging churches. These clearly divergent viewpoints could

Robin Scroggs, author of *Paul for a New Day* (Philadelphia: Fortress Press, 1977), is the Edward Robinson Professor of Biblical Theology at Union Theological Seminary in New York City.

not be reconciled nor could one cancel out the other. Given both kinds of statements, then, the problem was to piece together, with limited evidence, a plausible historical framework that could explain how such opposing stands existed within churches separated by such limited geographical distance and so few decades.

During these twenty-five years, much work has been done to try to unearth and interpret evidence of the acceptance within the earliest churches of greater equality and independence of its female members than was previously assumed. The scholarship is ongoing. Consensus has not yet emerged about many things because of the nature of the data itself. Some things, however, are beginning to be clearer. The following sketch lays out what seems to be in general acceptable to many scholars. We cannot know how this picture will be sharpened and colored by future interpretation, but what we do know now may lead to even greater awareness of the importance and power of women in the early church.

The Earliest Decades

Our earliest literary evidence for the church is, of course, the letters of Paul. While no such thing as certainty can exist in the historical reconstruction of the ancient world, there is consensus in nonconservative circles that we have probably seven authentic letters of Paul in our canon (1 Thessalonians, Galatians, Philippians, 1 and 2 Corinthians, Philemon and Romans). These authentic letters were perhaps all written within a period of seven or eight years of one another, during the decade of the 50s. (1 Thessalonians is a possible exception.)

By that decade the church had been in existence for nearly twenty years and had marched the road from the back hills of Galilean Palestine to the major cities of the Greco-Roman world. This movement represents a nearly unbelievable change in the cultural, sociological and political situation of the churches — and thus in the forms and expressions of the emerging faith. About this process we know very little. By the time of our known and still existing letters of Paul, the changes are already in place, and any clear correlation between the Greek church and the Palestinian communities is, at least in my judgment, mostly missing. We thus begin our story where we have to, knowing that it is not the real beginning.

Women in the Greek Churches

When one looks at these authentic letters of Paul (thus ignoring the later writings *attributed* to Paul, of Colossians, Ephesians and the Pastorals: 1 and 2 Timothy and Titus), a clear picture emerges of the exercise of participation, power and leadership by women within the communities of faith. Were we to guide ourselves by the circle of the Pauline missionary team, which was almost entirely male, we would be misled. And it is true that the names of men outnumber those of women. Nevertheless, women appear as full participants in many places.

Romans 16 provides remarkable evidence of the leadership role of women in the churches of this period.[1] Here a number of people are greeted (nineteen as individuals, either named or specifically referred to); the situation indicates that all of them are in one geographical locale. The chapter begins (vv. 1f.) with a commendation of Phoebe, who is said to be a *diakonos* of the church at Cenchreae and a benefactor (*prostatis*). Whether these are technical terms denoting office or not, they indicate that she exercises leadership roles. She is likely to be the one who is delivering Paul's letter to the church he is addressing, and it is equally likely that she is performing some service in the Pauline mission.[2]

Prisca and her husband Aquila are then mentioned as important co-workers with Paul (16:3f.). They host a church in their house (v. 5). Acts mentions them as Christian teachers and co-workers with Paul (Acts 18:2f., 18, 26), and Paul refers to them again (1 Cor. 16:19) as hosts of a church that meets in their home. Obviously both exercised leadership roles in several churches — Corinth, Ephesus and perhaps Rome as well.

Mary, said to be a hard worker, is listed in verse 6; verse 7 lists a person whose name is probably Junia, thus a woman, a leader who has been imprisoned for the faith and is called a prominent apostle.[3] In verse 12, three female workers are mentioned: Tryphaena, Tryphosa and Persis. While three other women

---

1. Scholars are uncertain whether chap. 16 is part of the original letter to the Romans or whether it is a fragment of a letter Paul addressed to some other congregation, perhaps at Ephesus. For our purposes it makes no difference.

2. If chapter 16 is addressed to Rome, it may be that Phoebe is sent ahead to prepare for Paul's hoped-for mission to Spain (see Rom. 15:23f). See R. Jewett, "Paul, Phoebe, and the Spanish Mission," in *The Social World of Formative Christianity and Judaism: Essays in Tribute to Howard Clark Kee*, ed. J. Neusner et al. (Philadelphia: Fortress, 1988), 142–61.

3. Grammatically the name could be either feminine or masculine, but the name as masculine is apparently not known in any extant Greek text, while the feminine is a common name.

are named in this chapter, they are not explicitly said to be workers in the church. But that seven women are singled out as workers, deacon and apostle within the confines of one chapter and one church shows the frequency of women in leadership roles.

Once elsewhere Paul refers by name to female church leaders. In Philippians 4:2f. he urges Euodia and Syntyche to "be of the same mind." Whether this implies a dispute between the two or not (the Greek is ambiguous), they are said to be co-workers with Paul for the gospel.

These instances are expressed by Paul in such a way as to indicate that he sees nothing unusual about female leadership, nor does he imply that female leadership is somehow subordinate to male leadership. He writes, rather, in such a way as to indicate that equality in leadership is a given and accepted reality in the Greek churches.

Important further evidence appears in 1 Corinthians 11:2–16. Here it is essential to separate the situation at Corinth as assumed by the text from what the text says about Paul's response to that situation. Liturgical moments in that church take the form of free and unstructured participation by individuals. Members led by the spirit stand to prophesy, speak in tongues, sing, etc. (see 1 Cor. 14:26–33). Women actively participate in this liturgical activity (1 Cor. 11:5); they pray and prophesy — and these activities are close to what we might understand today as leading the liturgy and preaching. That is, in the Corinthian church it seems ordinary that women participate equally with men in the worship services. By apparently denying the distinction between male and female dress, they further symbolize the equality they possess in Christ to perform any role within the church.

Paul himself, at least in this passage, clearly accepts the practice, although he wishes to alter the "dress code" of the women performing such functions. Nowhere in this section does he give any indication that he thinks such activity is inappropriate. It is simply part of the ordinary liturgical practice of the Greek church (as Paul implies in v. 16).

In a recent work, Antoinette Clark Wire has argued that the role of these women prophets at Corinth is larger than is usually assumed. She thinks that they are a numerous and influential subcommunity in the church. They have withdrawn from sexual relations, "moving the focus of their commitment to the new community." Their theology centers in affirmation of the present gifts of God. They "claim direct access to resurrected life in Christ through

God's spirit."[4] Freedom from restrictions and acceptance of variety of expression are marks of their faith. Whether Wire's judgments can be sustained in general seems uncertain to me. The significance of her work, however, must not be underplayed. She has indicated how one may read 1 Corinthians in a way that lends confidence in the picture of women actively participating in the life of the community and in its leadership.

What the dynamics were, whether social and/or theological, that led to this equality of participation — an equality that seems more realized in these communities than in most contemporary Jewish or Greco-Roman communities — cannot be recovered. What can be pointed to, however, is that this equality is clearly stated in what is rightly seen as a baptismal formula cited by Paul in Galatians 3: 26–28:

> For in Christ Jesus you are all children of God through faith. As many of you as were baptized into Christ have clothed yourselves with Christ. There is no longer Jew or Greek, there is no longer slave or free, there is no longer male and female; for all of you are one in Christ Jesus. [5]

The significance of this passage as a liturgical formula is immense. It shows that this is not an isolated statement by Paul but a faith common to the Greek churches, at least those in the Pauline circle. Here entrance into the community of faith is said to abolish at least the value judgments placed on these statuses in the outside world. Within the church Jew and Greek are equal, as are also slave and free, male and female. That this was no mere theoretical assertion is evidenced by what we have already seen — the freedom of women to exercise active participation and leadership in the communities.

Paul

The evidence above is all drawn from the Pauline letters and can be assessed independently of Paul's own judgments. Since Paul has become an authoritative figure, due to the weight of the canon, it is important to evaluate his own attitudes, even if they would represent but one man's opinion, within the actual practice of the churches.

---

4. Antoinette Wire, *The Corinthian Women Prophets* (Minneapolis: Fortress, 1990), 182, 185.

5. See R. Scroggs, "Paul and the Eschatological Woman," *Journal of the American Academy of Religion* 40 (1972): 291–92; H. D. Betz, *Galatians* (Philadelphia: Fortress, 1979), 181–85; Ben Witherington III, *Women in the Earliest Churches* (Cambridge: Cambridge University Press, 1988).

But what is his attitude? In recent years this has been variously assessed, from judgment that Paul approves and supports this equality to the opposite conclusion that he is interested in suppressing such equality in favor of a more conventional order and a theology of submission.[6] In what follows I will argue that Paul not only accepts this freedom but supports it (with some qualifications); indeed, I believe that his basic theology requires him to support it and has perhaps forced him to rethink his prejudice that the male is superior.

The information described above in itself says much about Paul's acceptance of the practices of women's leadership. Nowhere does he argue against it, and more than once he speaks warmly of the women co-workers in his mission activity (e.g., Phil. 4:2f.; Rom. 16:1f.).

He not only cites the baptismal formula of equality in Galatians 3:26–28, but he also seems to support that equality in marital relations. 1 Corinthians 7 is a section of text in which Paul is answering probably several questions put to him by the Corinthians concerning marital relations, including sexual activity and divorce. As is frequently noted, he addresses both women and men in this section and affirms equally their rights and responsibilities.[7] Both have the same responsibility for sexual communication in marriage; both have the same responsibilities concerning divorce. Paul's traditional (in his case, Jewish) male attitudes are here surely captured by his understanding of the gospel and radically rerouted.

The section in 1 Corinthians 11:2–16 raises more problems, in part because the passage is obscure in a number of respects. While Paul accepts the validity of liturgical leadership of women, he couches his address in language that attempts to differentiate sharply one sex from another and, on the surface at least, seems to assume a hierarchy of value in which woman is subordinate to man. This happens in two ways.

1. He says man is the head of the woman, while man's head is Christ (v. 3). Traditionally this has been taken to mean the subordinate nature of woman to man. Such a view is not without its difficulties. For one thing, Paul nowhere else makes such a judgment. For another, toward the end of the section he concludes that male and female are mutually interdependent (vv. 11f.). An alternative

---

6. For the former see my article, "Paul and the Eschatological Woman"; for the latter, Wire, *The Corinthian Women Prophets.*

7. See Scroggs, "Paul and the Eschatological Woman," 294–96; Witherington, *Women in the Earliest Churches,* 26f.; Wire, *The Corinthian Women Prophets,* 81f. Wire comes to a less sanguine conclusion about the reason for Paul's structure here.

translation of the Greek word *kephale* ("head") has been proposed that has much to recommend it. In Greek *kephale* is not normally used as a metaphor to refer to superior status or authority. Instead, the word may mean "source," in which case Paul would be referring to the Genesis narrative in which woman is created out of man (Gen. 2:22f.). Thus Paul in 1 Corinthians 11:3 may be interpreting this narrative.[8] If this interpretation is rejected, as it frequently is, then it seems that Paul's Jewish heritage has suddenly taken charge of his usual acceptance of the equality of male and female. I find this unlikely.

2. Paul insists, irascibly and dogmatically, on some sort of head covering for the women leaders when performing liturgical functions. His language and meaning are so obscure at this point that it is not possible to be sure even what kind of dress is meant, much less just why Paul thinks it important. He obviously wants to distinguish the dress of male and female but is not able to describe cogently or clearly his reasons. We have to remain with the basic affirmation that Paul accepts the equality of women in leadership roles but feels it necessary to insist on dress distinctions. While this may have been felt as an unfair limitation by the women in Corinth, it does not seem to me that Paul believes he is infringing on their right to perform leadership roles in any way.

The most difficult passage in the authentic Pauline letters is, without doubt, 1 Corinthians 14:33b–35.

> As in all the churches of the saints, women should be silent in the churches. For they are not permitted to speak, but should be subordinate, as the law also says. If there is anything they desire to know, let them ask their husbands at home. For it is shameful for a woman to speak in church.

This seems to take back everything Paul has accepted in 1 Corinthians 11:2–16 and elsewhere. For how can women perform leadership roles, especially liturgical, if they do not speak? That is, on the surface it baldly contradicts what Paul said a few paragraphs earlier in his letter. Not surprisingly, scholars have exercised much imagination to try to square the circle (or circle the square).

1. Many have tried to find an interpretation of the material in chapter 14 that does not contradict Paul's earlier acceptance in chapter 11. Simply put, the attempt is made to find a *kind* of speaking

---

8. See Scroggs, "Paul and the Eschatological Woman," 298f.; Scroggs, "Paul and the Eschatological Woman: Revisited," *JAAR* 42 (1974): 534f.; Witherington, *Women in the Earliest Churches*, 84f.

that is different from the inspired speech implied in chapter 11. Most recently, Ben Witherington represents this approach. For him, the speech in chapter 14 refers to a questioning of what was said in the worship service, perhaps judging of the prophecy or some other speaking done by others in the assembly.[9]

2. Elisabeth Schüssler Fiorenza finds consonance in the two chapters by distinguishing between the women addressed. In 1 Corinthians 11, holy women who are unmarried and who do perform liturgical roles are addressed; in chapter 14, on the other hand, the women are married and nonparticipatory in the liturgical rites. It is the second category of women who are not to ask questions in church.[10]

3. Antoinette Clark Wire overcomes the seeming contradiction by claiming that the passage in 1 Corinthians 14 is what Paul *really* means. It is a final judgment denying women the right he has, for tactical purposes, conceded in chapter 11. What Paul wants is for women of any sort in any way to cease speaking in liturgical settings.[11]

4. Another possibility is that 1 Corinthians 14:33b–35 is an insertion by a later Christian into Paul's letter, at the time the letter was being edited for publication.[12] While this may seem a counsel of desperation, it is perhaps less so than those attempts to explain such seemingly contradictory material as the work of one writer. In my judgment, no suggestion that has been put forward to reconcile the passages makes sufficient sense, unless Paul is a schizophrenic. Furthermore, the location in the manuscript tradition of the passage in more than one place and the use of language in ways atypical of Paul lend support to the hypothesis that this passage was later inserted into the text.[13] The language and content of the passage are remarkably close to those in the Pastorals (1 and 2 Timothy and Titus, considered to be by another, later author). Thus I believe the best argument is that this passage is a later insert. In this case, the passage needs to be interpreted as part of the change in thinking

9. Witherington, *Women in the Earliest Churches*, 90–104.

10. Elisabeth Schüssler Fiorenza, *In Memory of Her* (New York: Crossroad, 1984), 230–32.

11. Wire, *The Corinthian Women Prophets*, 149–58.

12. It is widely thought that 1 Corinthians, as well as 2 Corinthians, is made up of parts of several letters and edited by an unknown scribe, perhaps toward the beginning of the second century. The scribe could easily insert material into such a composite document, not written by Paul (as, e.g., 2 Cor. 6:14–7:1).

13. See Scroggs, "Paul and the Eschatological Woman," 284; C. K. Barrett, *A Commentary on the First Epistle to the Corinthians* (New York: Harper & Row, 1968), 330–33.

evidenced in some later New Testament documents, especially the Pastorals.

For someone like myself who believes that theological convictions do indeed influence thought, perhaps the most telling argument that Paul is in basic agreement with the Greek church is the crucial harmony between the equality expressed in the baptismal formula (Gal. 3:26–28) and his theology of justification by grace. If God completely and universally accepts people without qualification — the deepest meaning of justification by grace — then all are equal before God. Distinctions still exist, but the valuations people have put on such distinctions are destroyed. Since all are equal before God, all are equal before one another, no matter how strong or weak, how talented or simple, or how status-valued they have been. Thus Paul's stress on freedom and equality is a necessary corollary of his theological heart of hearts. If he had not accepted the equality of male and female, he would have contradicted the deepest dimension of his faith in God's act in Christ.[14]

I conclude that Paul stands firmly within the tradition of the Greek church in accepting the equality of male and female. Paul is human, finite and imperfect, no doubt. We see rough and occasionally raw edges showing through. Yet it is highly likely that basically Paul affirms the realization of the baptismal formula and lives out of it in his relations with other women and men. Paul's greatest contribution, however, does not lie in his acceptance of a situation of liberation he inherited, but in the theological rationale he provided, a rationale that still lies at the heart of the Christian church's affirmation that in Christ male and female are equal. Without such rationale, the church's struggle for equality will always remain ambiguous and incomplete.

The Later New Testament Decades

If the churches had remained true to this realized vision of the earliest Greek church, would the long, tragic story of the repression of women in the history of the West have been necessary? Sadly, this vision flickered so briefly. By the middle of the second century of our era, it was extinguished in the churches that would become orthodox, if perhaps still aflame in churches that were or would be dubbed heretical. In fact, the change began only a few decades after Paul. The irony is that it began and was strengthened by appeal

---

14. See Scroggs, *Paul for a New Day* (Philadelphia: Fortress, 1977), 14–20; 42–48.

to his authority — through the writing of documents in his name. Paul has still not lived down his false reputation. I shall now briefly chronicle the return to oppressive male-female relationships.[15]

Sadly, it is in the deutero-Pauline tradition (the later letters attributed to but probably not written by Paul) that this reversal is most obviously present. In Colossians, Ephesians and 1 Peter (a document which, despite its name, seems theologically within the deutero-Pauline tradition) are found descriptions of the proper familial relationships. The phrase applied to the wife's relation to the husband is the same in all three letters: "wives, be subject to your husbands, as is fitting in the Lord" (Col. 3:18); "wives, be subject to your husbands as you are to the Lord" (Eph. 5:22); "wives...accept the authority of your husbands" (1 Pet. 3:1 — here the Greek verb is the same as in the first two passages, despite differences in the NRSV translation). Because these passages apply to familial relationships, they do not help ascertain what the fate of female leadership roles in the churches might have been.

In still later Pauline tradition, the Pastorals suggest that women are being excluded from leadership roles they once enjoyed. The most startling passage occurs in 1 Timothy 2:11–15:

> Let a woman learn in silence with full submission. I permit no woman to teach or to have authority over a man; she is to keep silent. For Adam was formed first, then Eve, and Adam was not deceived, but the woman was deceived and became a transgressor. Yet she will be saved through childbearing, provided they continue in faith and love and holiness, with modesty.

Here is a formal rejection of the authority of women in leadership roles, at least leadership roles in relation to males. Indeed the woman's function is now reduced to childbearing and rearing. The statement is harsh; her salvation depends — if one takes the text literally — not upon her own piety but upon her success in raising her children so that they become pious.

In other places, the Pastorals may refer to church roles for women. It is possible, but I think unlikely, that the reference to women in 1 Timothy 3:11 may refer to women who are deacons. It is also possible that the word translated "older women" in Titus 2:3 may refer to female presbyters, but if so, their teaching authority is directed solely or primarily to the teaching of other women (v. 4).

---

15. For a statement of this change, see my articles in *The Interpreter's Dictionary of the Bible, Supplementary Volume* (Nashville: Abingdon, 1976) on "Marriage in the New Testament" and "Women in the New Testament."

An order of widows seems to be recognized in 1 Timothy 5:3–16; a formal enrollment is pointed to, and distinctions made as to who may be enrolled.[16] Their task is said to be to do good works, bring up children, show hospitality, wash the feet of the saints and help the afflicted (v. 10). Schüssler Fiorenza comments about the situation assumed in the Pastorals: "Leading women are still permitted to teach, but their teaching is now restricted to the instruction of other women."[17]

There is another side, however, to this picture, although inevitably much less sharply focused. The Pastorals are in part polemical literature, and by reading between the lines, one can get some sense of the opposition. One simple approach is to say that when a prohibition is laid down, it is because someone is doing what that rule wishes to prohibit. Thus if the author of 1 Timothy prohibits women from having authority over men, it must mean that somewhere such authority is being exercised. But where?

Second Timothy may give some hint. In 3:1–9 a group is attacked who must be Christian, since they are said to hold "to the outward form of godliness" (v. 5). One of their (no doubt successful) activities is to "make their way into households and captivate silly women, overwhelmed by their sins and swayed by all kinds of desires, who are always being instructed and can never arrive at a knowledge of the truth" (vv. 6f.). If we "translate" the polemic, it seems clear that the opposition is conducting a successful mission among the women of the community. First Timothy 4:1–3 adds to the picture by identifying this group as ascetics who forbid marriage and certain foods.

If it is fair to put all of these hints together, a picture emerges of a church in which women exercise the same leadership roles as did women in the earlier decades. Furthermore, they practice an ascetic life, including abstinence from marriage and sexuality. Leadership and sexual abstinence are here linked together. In the process of condemning such leadership, the Pastorals then link a positive view of marriage and sexuality to the subordination of women to men. The petty bitterness expressed by the author of 2 Timothy suggests that those whom he attacks are having more missionary success among women than he is. Women seem to be finding more fulfillment in the other communities.

The uneasily held tension of equality *and* marriage visible in

---

16. See the discussion in David Verner, *The Household of God: The Social World of the Pastoral Epistles* (Chicago: Scholars Press, 1983).

17. Schüssler Fiorenza, *In Memory of Her,* 290.

some places in the earliest church is here dissolved in different ways in the Pastorals and their opposition respectively. Marriage now implies the subordination of women. Equality for women can happen only if they remain single. Where would Paul have fit in this scheme? No doubt he would have tried to bring the positions together under the rubric of justification by grace; but if he had had to decide, I think he would have placed himself in the camp of "the enemy" rather than in that of the one who wrote in his name.

Conclusions

I have tried to sketch the position taken in the earliest decades by the Greek church and the change in that position observable in the later deutero-Pauline writings. This no doubt simplistic sketch needs to be put in context by a few considerations.

1. Even the sparse data we have about the New Testament church shows that any simple developmental scheme is questionable. Churches existed in many different places with different viewpoints. If one could know the entire situation, it is likely that at any given point of time, one would find a number of views represented, some of them in conflict with others. The author of Luke-Acts, writing about the time of the Pastorals, may imply that in his view women should still exercise leadership roles. As well as I can determine, however, the before-after framework I have given works reasonably well for at least the churches in the Pauline tradition. And at some point the subordinationist stance of the deutero-Pauline letters became the orthodox view of the great church. The general movement from equality to subordinationism in the Pauline tradition thus may well reflect the movement in other churches that would come to represent "orthodoxy."

2. I have not tried to suggest why the change took place. Here one enters the realm of speculation — and although some very intelligent speculation has been suggested, it remains just that. Perhaps the most common view is that the movement toward subordination is part of the need to accommodate to the standards of the world around the communities. As the church became more noticed by that world, it was important to defuse antagonism and suspicion by showing that the church met the norm of the usual social standards. A community of equals (and not just male and female) would have been looked at with great anxiety by local governments and by Rome.

There is probably much truth in this speculation, but it does not get to the heart of the problem. After all, if our reading is right regarding the churches that the Pastoral author opposed, there *were* churches that did not feel they had to accommodate to societal standards and that went their way, perhaps courageously in the face of increasing societal opposition. What gave these churches their courage? Alas, an unanswerable question.

The question could be turned around. What happened in the churches of the Pastorals to make them *lose their courage?* I have a suggestion, no less speculative than others. I argued above that Paul gave a profound theological grounding to equality by his understanding of justification by grace. If one lives out of that sign of the gospel, one is compelled toward a practice of equality, since that is a necessary corollary. Is it significant that in the Pastorals, as well as in Colossians and Ephesians, the basic motif of Paul receives at best only lip-service? Certainly the motif is lost as the heart of one's relationship to God and thus to neighbor. When the dynamic grounding of one's faith disappears, it becomes easier to conform to pressures from outside.

However that may be, in the later orthodox church, the Pastorals were held to represent the true position about the place of women in church and society. They were at the same time the perspective from which Paul and his theology was viewed and interpreted. Only occasionally, and for brief periods of time, was Paul's theological heart resurrected, and only in most recent times have we begun to see what views of equality for women and men the earliest church proclaimed and lived.

PART TWO

The Church in Transition: Women's Re-Entry

◊

This is one of the most difficult sections of this book to shape. So much has happened in regard to the church's response to women's concerns in the last quarter of the century that it is impossible to do justice to it all. We have begun to think differently about theology; about language about God and people; about liturgy, worship and the spiritual dimension of all of life; about church architecture and the use of space; about church education, church leadership and authority; and finally about how we relate to one another in community.

The collection of material in this section provides illustrations of how the church's self-perception is changing. The material presented here is only illustrative, not exhaustive. But there is enough here to provide rich reasons for dialogue as well as motivation to expand the ways local churches participate in the life of the people of God.

SC

◇ **6** ◇

What Sins Should
Women Confess?

VALERIE SAIVING

The following excerpt is from a longer essay by Valerie Saiving, which appeared originally in 1960 in the *Journal of Religion*. It was one of the earlier watershed pieces by a woman theologian, examining traditional concepts of love and sin.

Saiving's thesis is that when the human condition is seen primarily from the male point of view, the resultant perception of sin as "pride" and "will-to-power" normally does not apply to women, whose major sin may very well be their self-denial, which they already practice to a fault.   *SC*

◇

IT IS MY CONTENTION that there are significant differences between masculine and feminine experience and that feminine experience reveals in a more emphatic fashion certain aspects of the human situation which are present but less obvious in the experience of men.

. . .

A mother who rejoices in her maternal role — and most mothers do most of the time — knows the profound experience of self-transcending love. But she knows, too, that it is not the whole meaning of life. For she learns not only that it is impossible to sustain a perpetual I-Thou relationship but that the attempt to do so

From Valerie Saiving, "The Human Situation: A Feminine View," *Journal of Religion* 40, no. 2 (April 1960): 100–112.

can be deadly. The moments, hours and days of self-giving must be balanced by moments, hours and days of withdrawal into, and enrichment of, her individual selfhood if she is to remain a whole person. She learns, too, that a woman can give too much of herself, so that nothing remains of her own uniqueness; she can become merely an emptiness, almost a zero, without value to herself, to [others], perhaps even to God.

For the temptations of woman as *woman* are not the same as the temptations of man as *man*, and the specifically feminine forms of sin — "feminine" not because they are confined to women or because women are incapable of sinning in other ways but because they are outgrowths of the basic feminine character structure — have a quality that can never be encompassed by such terms as "pride" and "will-to-power." They are better suggested by such terms as triviality, distractibility and diffuseness; lack of an organizing center or focus; dependence on others for one's own self-definition; tolerance at the expense of standards of excellence; inability to respect the boundaries of privacy; sentimentality, gossipy sociability and mistrust of reason — in short, underdevelopment or negation of the self.

This list of specifically feminine sins could be extended. All of them, however, are to be understood as merely one side of the feminine coin. For just as man's distance from nature is the precondition of his creativity, on the one hand, and his self-concern, on the other, so does woman's closeness to nature have dipolar potentialities. Her sureness of her own femininity and thus of her secure place in the scheme of things may, if she accepts the feminine role with joy, enable her to be a source of strength and refreshment to her husband, her children and the wider community.

If she has been brought up to devalue her femininity, on the other hand, this same sense that for her "anatomy is destiny" may create an attitude of stolid and sterile resignation, a feeling that there is no use in trying. Again, the fact that her whole growth toward womanhood has the character of an inevitable process of bodily maturation rather than that of a challenge and a task may lead her to dissipate herself in activities that are merely trivial. Yet it is the same lack of creative drive that may make it possible for her to perform cheerfully the thousand-and-one routine tasks — the woman's work that is never done — that someone must do if life is to go on. Her capacity for surrendering her individual concerns in order to serve the immediate needs of others...can, on the other hand, induce a kind of diffuseness of purpose, a tendency toward being easily distracted, a failure to discriminate between the more and the less important and an inability to focus in a sustained manner on the pursuit of any single goal. Her receptivity to the moods and feelings of others and her tendency to merge her selfhood in the joys, sorrows, hopes and problems of those around her are the positive expressions of an aspect of the feminine character that may also take the negative forms of gossipy sociability, dependence on others (such as husband or children) for the definition of her values or a refusal to respect another's right to privacy. And her capacity for forgiving love, for cherishing all her children equally,...can also express itself in a kind of indiscriminate tolerance that suspects or rejects all objective criteria of excellence.

All this is not meant to constitute an indictment of the feminine character as such. I have no wish, certainly, to add to the burden of guilt that has been heaped upon women — by themselves as well as by men — for centuries. My purpose, indeed, as far as it concerns women in particular, is quite the opposite. It is to awaken theologians to the fact that the situation of women, however similar it may appear on the surface of our contemporary world to the situation of man and however much it may be echoed in the life of individual men, is, at bottom, quite different — that the specifically feminine dilemma is, in fact, precisely the opposite of the masculine.

Today, when for the first time in human history it really seems possible that those endless housewifely tasks — which, along with the bearing and rearing of children, have always been enough to fill the whole of each day for the average woman — may virtually be eliminated; today, when at last women might seem to be in a position to begin to be both feminine and fully developed creative human beings; today, these same women are being subjected to pressures from many sides to return to the traditional feminine niche and to devote themselves wholly to the tasks of nurture, support and service of their families.

One might expect of theologians that they at least not add to these pressures. One might even expect them to support and encourage the woman who desires to be both a woman and an individual in her own right, a separate person some part of whose mind and feelings are inviolable, some part of whose time belongs strictly to herself, in whose house there is, to use Virginia Woolf's marvelous image, "a room of one's own." Yet theology, to the extent that it has defined the human condition on the basis of masculine experience, continues to speak of such desires as sin or temptation to sin. If such a woman believes the theologians, she will try to strangle those impulses in herself. She will believe that, having chosen marriage and children and thus being face to face with the needs of her family for love, refreshment and forgiveness, she has no right to ask anything for herself but must submit without qualification to the strictly feminine role. . . .

I do not think we can turn back this particular clock. Nor do I think that the feminine dilemma is of concern only to women. It is important for men, too, not only because it is a loss to every man when a woman fails to realize her full self-identity, but because there is, it seems to me, a growing trend in contemporary life toward the femininizing of society itself, including men as well as women.

Worship That Welcomes

Since Valerie Saiving wrote the preceding piece over thirty years ago, women have come a long way in claiming their capacity to perform with excellence in every field previously considered man's domain. But they have also made tremendous gains in reaffirming those particular feminine attributes that society as a whole failed to value. They have learned how to adapt the masculine "focused consciousness" to the task of interpreting their own "diffuse awareness of everything"[1] and in the process, they have begun to reaffirm this uniquely feminine consciousness that has always been theirs. They are also reaffirming the value of the many arts, skills and creative ways of doing things that have been a part of the woman's world for generations, but have often been devalued by the culture as a whole.

Out of their need to be included in the whole life of the church, women have begun to offer the church new ways of being and doing in the presence of God. The articles gathered in this chapter illustrate how language, space and patterns of worship are being reshaped, creating new comforts and discomforts for those who seek to worship God "in spirit and in truth."

How Do We Name Ourselves and God?

Who could have imagined thirty or forty years ago the progress we have made toward a more inclusive language for the people of God? The New Revised Standard Version of the Bible, issued in 1990, has made every effort to be inclusive of people without in any way distorting the original texts. The language about

---

1. Irene Claremont de Castillejo in *Knowing Woman* (New York: G. P. Putnam's Sons, 1973) uses these terms to describe differences in the way men and women perceive reality.

God is still predominantly masculine, but even there the scholars have been much more sensitive to those feminine images of God that do appear throughout the Bible, and they have been very careful to see that such images do not lose their significance in translation.

Several denominations have produced new hymnals in recent years that are more inclusive both in their language and in their racial and cultural range than their predecessors. The Inclusive Language Lectionary of Scripture passages for church services was published in the 1980s, and more and more resources are becoming available for churches so that those who really want to include the whole community in their worship can do so thoughtfully and graciously.

But sometimes our resistance to new patterns is more complex than just wanting or not wanting to change. Browne Barr observed:

> Many congregations' intense resistance to inclusive language does not mean that they are simply stiff necked. The roots of that resistance, acknowledged or not, lie very deep in religious experience. For words and other symbols are the lifeblood of the church. When we change words we invite a changed perception of the reality to which the words point. To demand that the words of faith change is to demand that one's faith change. And in changing it can either grow or shrivel, blossom or die....
>
> One important way of guarding against alienation is to take care that new, inclusive language does not call undue attention to itself. This is certainly possible to accomplish, but it does require much preparation and creativity. I have worked at such efforts myself. In revising some early sermons, I realized that they were much improved by translation into inclusive language. However, it is also clear that no one would be particularly aware of how they were improved; the revision does not scream out, "See how inclusive this language is!"[2]

SC

2. "Inclusive Language, Women's Ordination, and Another Great Awakening," *Christian Century* (April 13, 1988): 366–68.

◇

A New Language of Prayer

VIENNA COBB ANDERSON

A recently published resource that is beautifully inclusive is *Prayers of Our Hearts in Word and Action* by Vienna Cobb Anderson, rector of St. Margaret's Episcopal Church, Washington, D.C. In the introduction she speaks of the needs that led her to write. *SC*

MANY HAVE GROWN WEARY, as I have, of waiting a lifetime for the church to include the longings of our hearts in words that are inclusive and in liturgies that reflect the changes of our lives. Week after week, many of us have been burdened by the weight of a language that neither names our dreams, struggles or sorrows, nor offers us the consolation of feeling named or affirmed as full members of the Body of Christ.

Some individuals have left the community of the church; they think they have lost their faith since the language of worship seems so foreign to the longings, doubts and fears of their hearts. Others wouldn't dream of entering through the door, assuming that whatever happens inside is archaic and irrelevant to their own life experiences.

Indeed, to me the tragedy of liturgy today is that we have made the language of worship so abstract that it is nearly impossible to sense the joy and blessing of life in an earthy and real way. We neither laugh nor weep in church, and that is a great pity that robs us of a deeper compassion for others and diminishes our own living.

...During the period of sweeping liturgical change in all denominations during the 1960s and 1970s, words were shuffled on paper by scholars, but the cries of seekers for a new language of prayer went largely unheard.

It is to help in the process of filling this gap in our liturgical life that I have written [these] rituals and prayers.

From *Prayers of Our Hearts in Word and Action* by Vienna Cobb Anderson (New York: Crossroad, 1991), from the Introduction and p. 101.

Prayer to God

How do I name you,
when the words of tradition
speak of oppression,
abuse, and countless tears?
How do I name you,
when the words I seek
seem strange, empty,
and without history or feeling?
How do I name you, when you are beyond
naming, beyond knowing?
Yet name you I shall;
for you are my heart,
my life, my hope.
I shall name you
"the holy one who hears my cry,
understands my pain,
and loves me as I am."
To you I pray and give thanks.
So be it. Amen.

Church and Space: When Women Dream

When women dream of space for worship and creative learning, they often imagine configurations quite different from those found in most of our traditional houses of worship. And the space they imagine is much more compatible with their way of leading and participating in worship. Traditionally, our churches have been designed by men; and they have reflected masculine understandings of power and authority, of grandeur and glory.

Many of us belong to, or occasionally worship in, large churches of Romanesque or Gothic architecture. Huge as these cathedral-like spaces are, we feel embraced by them and nurtured by their majestic, story-telling stained glass windows and by their rich array of wood and stone sculpture of both human and angelic figures. We not only want to enjoy them ourselves, we want to preserve them for generations to come.

And yet, to stand in the pulpit of such a place is to know that it was designed with men in mind, not women. When

choir and clergy process up the aisle of the nave on a Sunday morning, the impression is that they are going up and
up and up — to Jerusalem? To the Temple? To the place of
power and authority? To the place where one must stand in
grand elevation and call out to the congregation, "Come, let us
worship"?

Though modern technology has made it possible for
women's voices to be heard even in such spaces as these,
women think quite differently, most of the time, about space
and their place in it. Because they so often think of shared
leadership and shared responsibility, they are much more likely
to dream of space in circular, intimate terms.

In a book titled *Women-Church,*[1] Rosemary Radford Ruether
writes of groups of women who often gather in each other's
houses to talk about and experience new ways of being the
church. In a sense, these house meetings are an expression of
the same kind of unrest that gave birth to the missionary societies of the nineteenth century. Then, women felt marginal to
the church's mission so they found a way of being involved.
When today's women feel marginal to the church's worship
and way of being in the world, some gather to talk about
and experience new ways of worship that seem to connect
with their deep longings for community with one another and
communion with God.

They design and experience worship that uses inclusive
language and hymns that relate to women's experiences as
well as men's; worship that examines the Scriptures from a
woman's perspective and that includes prayers that connect
with women's reality; worship that involves movement as well
as word and song. And though they usually meet anywhere
that is convenient, they now meet at all levels of the church's
life, whether in the local community or at a worldwide gathering of church representatives, such as the World Council of
Churches' Seventh Assembly in Canberra, Australia, in January
of 1991.

There, they erected a tent called WomenSpace where

---

1. See Rosemary Radford Ruether, *Women-Church: Theology and Practice of
Feminist Liturgical Communities* (San Francisco: Harper & Row, 1985), 146–47.
"Women-Church" is a term used by contemporary Christian women to describe
alternative ways of being in Christian community. Often such groups are made up
only of women who meet periodically to express together what they feel is missing
in the communions to which they now belong. See the excerpt from *Birthing and
Blessing* on p. 71 as another expression of such an alternative.

women from every continent held a Pre-Assembly meeting, convening around such concerns as the plight of Aboriginal Women of Australia (in which they had opportunities to experience firsthand the insights and celebrations of these women whose ancestors were Australia's first inhabitants); Women, Health and Wholeness; Children of the World; Women, Peace and Violence, and Women Renewing Creation. Other gatherings included discussions of theology and feminism; a Eucharist led by women; song, dance, and meditation.

In such gatherings, women often discuss what to them would be an appropriate church architecture, in contrast to our traditional church buildings. Ruether writes of a retreat center, envisioned by women. This is a place not so much like a "church building" as we think of churches today as it is like a celebration center, using celebration in its liturgical sense of being a place to celebrate God's presence in our midst. Such a center is envisioned as a place of worship, renewal, rest and retreat that might be available to anybody — families, young and old, people of many cultures and backgrounds.

> I envision various purposes of such a center. One space that is needed is a place for liturgies that is both centering and elevating. I envision a round room able to hold as many as 150 people, but comfortable with only a dozen or so. It would have no immovable furniture and so could be adapted to various types of gatherings: conferences and talks, collective meals and liturgies. It would have a dome of natural light in the center of the ceiling and panels of colored glass in rainbow hues around this center, standing for the plurality and unity of all good things in creation. There would also be narrow tall windows around the circumference of the wall. The building and windows would be oriented to catch the light at the winter and summer solstices.

Such a center, Ruether notes, might also include a smaller circular chamber for those profoundly intimate services related to birth and death, where family and close friends bond together to express joy and grief and to seek that special consolation that comes through the gathered community responding to the sacredness of life.

There might also be a space that would include some of the elements we might now find in an educational wing of a church, but perhaps designed more like a retreat center than a "school plant." A place where meals could be prepared and served, a space for a garden, perhaps a pool, all enclosed in a dome-like structure with a glass ceiling to bring in the natural sunlight.

> The celebration center should, ideally, be set in some area of pleasant meadows and woods. It would have several small cottages scattered about, with sleeping and creating spaces....A circular outdoor meadow area for... celebrations...would also be desirable. The land should have an outdoor pool of water or a running stream. The cottages can also be used for extending the functions of the center, such as providing a play center for children, a weaving or pottery center or a library.

Extravagant dreaming for such times as these? Yes, in a way, but even when our dreams are unrealistic, they release the imagination so that we can ask revitalizing questions about the purpose of church, the shape a church environment for learning, for growth, for community, for worship.

One minister recently observed that when his congregation decided to build a new church, it was assumed that the women would be involved in planning the kitchen; the rest of the structure would be left to the men. What if, when congregations decide to build or add to their church structures, they began to involve women, too, as architects, as interior decorators, as teachers, as parents, as persons who spend a lot of their time thinking about the relationship of space to community and communication and, yes, to congregational worship?

SC

◊

Where Hospitality Welcomes

SUSAN BLAINE, ROBERT SEAVER
and JANET WALTON

A few years ago, Union Theological Seminary, in the vanguard
of a movement that was taking place in seminaries and local
churches across the country, redesigned its worship space by
removing all the bolted-down pews, furnishing it so that everything in that space was moveable. Today the chapel can be
designed anew for every occasion if the people desire.   SC

◊

AN EXAMPLE of the active engagement of art and worship in such a
space occurred when a group of women students planned the opening worship for women's history week. They invited the community
to experience worship as seeking after God in the ordinary, everyday
processes of life. This immanent God, known where two or three are
gathered, incarnated where hospitality welcomes, lives where gossip
in its oldest sense flourishes. "Gossip," from the Old English *God-
sibbe*, meaning God's wisdom, is heard in the talk of women —
in recipes, advice, consolation, sympathy, help passed across the
kitchen table and around the sewing circle. God is known in the
ordinary, day-to-day work of building up life.

To help open the way to this experience of God, the planners
employed the tradition of women's folk art. Folk artists are, by and
large, ordinary people who combine skill and imagination to transform common materials into items of beauty. They work generally in
intimate, collaborative settings. Their art is functional — items such
as quilts and rugs, needed for use in everyday life.

The worship planners transformed James Chapel into a folk
artist's studio. They devised small "sewing circles" seating eight to
ten people. Each circle had a table of simple materials: bright fab-
rics, colored pens, scissors, pins, tape. Because folk art is useful, the
planners endowed this artistic endeavor with a special purpose by
inviting the community to participate in the peace ribbon movement that was then being organized nationally. People across the

---

Adapted from an article that appeared in *Let the People Worship* (San
Carlos, Calif., Schuyler Institute for Worship and the Arts), 3 (Autumn
1988): 7–12.

U.S. were creating quilted panels depicting their desire to preserve life from nuclear destruction. The panels were to be joined into a large ribbon to encircle the Pentagon with visions of peace and hope during a demonstration later that year. Members of the planning team volunteered to bring Union's completed banners to that demonstration.

Worship began with a reading of the lectionary text for the week: 1 Corinthians 1:26 on the wisdom of God revealed in the foolish. Leaders then welcomed the congregation into the unusual space by inviting them to locate themselves, imaginatively, around a kitchen table, on the back porch, in the front parlor — into wherever women have met God as they gathered to carry on the foolish, ordinary business of building up life. They then explained the process and invited the people to begin.

The main portion of the service was spent in the small groups. Each group had a facilitator to help get things started, to clarify instructions, make suggestions, encourage the shy. Each group approached their task differently; some worked together on an overall design, individuals in other groups made separate contributions to a kind of crazy-quilt pattern. Groups seemed to begin tentatively but soon...the room buzzed as people worked, made suggestions, helped each other, laughed out loud at what was transpiring.

Toward the end of the service, the pianist began to play the tune "Jacob's Ladder," and the community was invited to sing new words: "sewing Sarah's circle." Two dancers went from group to group to collect the panels and show them around the room. The beauty and variety of what had been created in the short time won gasps, applause and laughter. One group wouldn't let go of its work and followed the dancer out of the circle dancing into the wider space, and others followed. Soon the whole room was moving — people singing, laughing, admiring the work they had accomplished.

A prayer of thanksgiving completed the service, but people lingered in the space, reluctant to leave. Something had happened. Artistic engagement had tapped the community's imagination and hope. We had contributed to a larger community's effort for peace. We had enjoyed one another in a space that felt cozy and safe. "I felt affirmed" said one student, a mother of four children. She, and others like her, experienced in this worship setting her often devalued work transformed when seen in its rightful context: the ordinary day-to-day revealed for what it is, the precious vehicle of the life of God.

◊

Women, Word and Song

ROSEMARY CATALANO MITCHELL
and GAIL ANDERSON RICCIUTI

Journalists sometimes say they tell one story that is a parable of many. In a sense, that is what the following article does. It tells how one local church began to expand the spiritual life of its people. It is a story of a church sensitive to the needs of women. Countless other local churches are doing similar things. We offer this story as an example only. Though it developed within one Reformed tradition, with certain modifications it could apply to any Christian communion or community.   *SC*

◊

IN MARGARET ATWOOD'S NOVEL *The Handmaid's Tale*, a repressive future society called Gilead keeps the Bible under lock and key. Only the commander of a household, a male, is permitted to read it — and then only selectively. Many portions are *never* read aloud and so have faded gradually from common memory. Women are not permitted to read at all.

The handmaid named Offred, whose stream of consciousness makes up the story's narrative, observes that "the Bible is kept locked up the way people once kept tea locked up — to keep the servants from stealing it.... The Bible is an incendiary device: who *knows* what we'd make of it, if we could get our hands on it."

And so it is with many women here and now who have begun to discover for ourselves a spirituality no longer kept under the lock and key of the traditional, [man-centered] scriptural interpretations of our childhood years in Sunday School. We are finding, as did the early church and then the church of the Reformation, the liberating and incendiary power of the Word.

The gathering called "Women, Word and Song" had its beginning at the Downtown United Presbyterian Church, Rochester, New York, in the fall of 1987. A group of young women of the congregation

Rosemary Catalano Mitchell and Gail Anderson Ricciuti are both pastors in a team of four for the Downtown United Presbyterian Church of Rochester, New York. This article is from the Introduction to their book, *Birthings and Blessings: Liberating Worship Services for the Inclusive Church* (New York: Crossroad, 1991), 11–15.

who had not found a niche in traditional church women's activities were seeking opportunities to gather for Bible study, reflection and community building. At the same time, we knew of women who had been alienated from the institutional church — some of them for long years — by their experience of the church's abuse of power or its patriarchal theology, and we longed for a way to offer an alternative model of worship and reflection that would welcome all these sisters "home" to a faith community together.

We began to realize that in spite of the rich history of suffragist and feminist ferment in our area (upstate New York) there did not exist a Protestant expression of worship that was women-directed and women-oriented as well as inclusive. We also saw a need for outreach to women who were unchurched or "formerly churched," who for many reasons no longer participated in traditional worship. The older women of the congregation were receptive to our ideas and delighted to be able to invite a wider community into involvement; and so with the blessing and sponsorship of our congregation's Presbyterian Women organization, "Women, Word and Song" was born.

Since that time, we have met approximately every eight weeks on Sunday evenings — not in a formal "worship space" but in the church parlor. Twenty-five women attended our first gathering to participate in an early-Advent reflection on birthing. Since then, the number of women who attend "Women, Word and Song" has tripled. They have represented congregations other than our own, members of other faiths and those with no church affiliation whatsoever, in addition to active church members. After that first gathering we invited participants to work with us on an ad hoc basis in planning and leadership; and they have become a rich wellspring. Together, we have developed a statement of purpose that continues to inform this spiritual birthing process. It guides us "to engage women in theological reflection and Bible study to [identify] the connection between our faith and our experience; to promote the leadership...[and] to call forth the creativity of women as we explore new forms of worship; to provide alternative Christian worship experiences within the context of the local congregation for women for whom traditional worship forms have become irrelevant, meaningless, or oppressive...."

Through it all, it has become increasingly apparent to us that women are eager to reflect upon theology and spirituality with one another. We are convinced that programs like ours are vital not only to the survival of the Christian church, but to its transformation; and we hope readers will agree and catch the vision of such ministry.

Although "Women, Word and Song" is still new among us, its roots are deep. The rich soil out of which it has sprung...is a contemporary experimental and experiential form of worship, which had its beginnings with the birth of the Downtown Church some eighteen years ago. Three downtown congregations, all within a radius of three city blocks, entered together into a thorough study/visioning process over the course of several years — deciding, as a result, to merge for the sake of wise stewardship, vital witness and mission in the city. It was a time of tremendous excitement. Out of that creative ferment came many new ideas — including the vision of "alternative" worship each Sunday morning planned by the people, growing out of their community life and in dialogue with Scripture. In nurturing the tender shoot from the older branch, we have learned that frontiers give birth to frontiers!

This experimental alternative worship, Celebration II, as it is called, has now journeyed and evolved through almost two decades, each Sunday morning service different from the week before and without a traditional setting, sermon or choir. The constant, however, has been the bringing together of all ages and abilities. Through this experience, an entire congregation — including those who choose to worship exclusively in the "traditional" Celebration I — has come to accept and expect diversity, creative theological inquiry and inclusiveness. And we believe that these qualities in worship and church life have nourished an excitement about the Bible as well as a maturity of faith and mission that are too often missing in many Protestant forms of worship.

. . .

Starting Points

Our "Women, Word and Song" gathering is rooted in feminist premises regarding worship. This is reflected in a diversity of style that stands in bold contrast to the traditional worship experience of many, if not most, churches. Common to the fabric of each of these services are foundational starting points — many of which have taken shape through the course of one congregation's life together and its commitment to the ministry of the whole people of God. We describe ten of them here, in order to offer to women and men in other faith communities a springboard for exploring creative vistas in their own worship life.

1. *Corporateness and Collegiality.* No single leader in the community is responsible for creating worship. Not only worshiping, but
also planning, are corporate acts, so there is a fluidity of leadership. In practice this means that a different core group of women is
intentionally brought together to plan each gathering.

2. *The Validity of the Experiential.* Our very life experience is holy!
This means that nothing is forbidden for discussion in the context
of worship and that the language of worship does not necessarily
have to be "worship language." In this respect, "Women, Word and
Song" is based upon the expectation that each woman has faith,
wisdom and insight worth sharing. Again, this stance enables spiritual leadership to flow back and forth throughout the worshiping
community.

3. *The Local Is the Universal.* Although part of the richness of
"Women, Word and Song" has been its inclusion of women from a
variety of backgrounds, the services have been created in the context
of a specific local church and its particular faith tradition. This has
been a marked contrast to most ecumenical or regional gatherings in
which the worship experience is often, of necessity, reduced to the
simplest common denominator.

4. *The Centrality of the Word.* While women of other traditions
have also created rituals, liturgies and prayer services with roots in
their own historic expression of faith, "Women, Word and Song" intentionally springs from the Reformed tradition, in that the Word
carries weight that anchors the entire service. It is our goal that the
biblical text is experienced not as an *addition* to worship, but as the
fertile ground out of which the full expression of worship grows.
Whereas the proclamation of God's Word in terms of preaching has
historically been the focus of Reformed worship, proclamation in the
context of "Women, Word and Song" takes many different forms.

5. *The Sensuality of Worship.* Worship invites the use of all the
senses, not only the auditory. We feel it is also important to be
conscious of the visual, tactile and olfactory and to allow time for
worshipers to savor these channels of spiritual nurture. Without
them, worship becomes arid — cut off from its richest depths.

6. *The Flexibility of Sacred Space.* The "sacred" dimension of life
is not confined exclusively to designated sanctuary spaces with standard accoutrements such as organ, pews, stained glass and pulpit.
Worship in a feminist mode blesses and finds blessing in *unexpected*
space such as parlor, lounge or entryway; where the breaking open
of old expectations and visual patterns allows for the in-breaking
of the Spirit — often with breathtaking insight! Each space has its

own feeling and unique possibilities for eliciting both reverence and interaction.

7. *The Significance of Rhythm.* We have happily freed ourselves from the assumption that worship of this kind must happen every week. Instead, a more flexible rhythm has allowed us to focus our gatherings around the seasons of life and liturgy, with time for a creative process that would be excluded by rigid scheduling.

8. *Variety in Worship Order.* Historically, our own tradition has valued the conduct of worship "decently and in order." While maintaining respect for that principle, we also affirm that many formats can exist together in the same worshiping community. Although each "Women, Word and Song" gathering incorporates various basic elements (song, prayer, engagement with the Word through Scripture and other writings, conversation and the sharing of life experience) the order and ways in which these are expressed vary a great deal from gathering to gathering.

9. *The Surprising Role of Worship Leaders.* The role of a worship leader in our celebrations contrasts with traditional expectations. To enable community members to follow the Spirit's movement among them, the leader must not so much talk as listen — at a level that, as theologian Nelle Morton wrote, will "hear them into speech." With this awareness, the leader's role is to remind the community that the Word of God does not originate from *her* but among *them.*

10. *The Wind of the Spirit.* Throughout this book we attempt to provide thorough and detailed notes on background, preparation and "choreography." Although the most subtle nuances of worship in *any* style ought to be carefully considered for the sake of aesthetic beauty as well as theological coherence, nevertheless in the last analysis it is the movement of the Holy Spirit that brings the hour of worship alive. Worship leaders must maintain a sense of humor and humility about this! The printed order of worship is best viewed not as a jungle gym on which to climb up unyielding bars, but as a flying trapeze — whose fluidity demands that we often let go and trust ourselves to the "air"! "The wind blows where it wills, and you hear the sound of it, but you do not know whence it comes or whither it goes; so it is with every one [and every experience of worship] born of the Spirit" (John 3:8). The sudden emergence of insight, laughter or tears is not viewed as disruptive to a well-ordered service, but a blessing sign. Those who learn to trust themselves to that flow will know worship as both a living and a life-giving moment!

◇ **8** ◇

Ordination from
the Woman's Perspective

BARBARA BROWN ZIKMUND

While the church continues to structure its life by hierarchical standards, not only is ordination for women a crucial issue, but also elected leadership in the various communions and in the national and world councils of such communions.

By 1990, the United Methodist Church had elected five women as bishops (three are active, one has retired, one has died) and the Episcopal Church had appointed its first woman bishop. But so far there are no women heads of communions.

The National Council of the Churches of Christ now has an ordained woman as its general secretary. (Joan Brown Campbell of the Disciples of Christ is the second woman to hold that position, the first being Presbyterian lay woman Claire Randall.) The World Council of Churches includes women among its elected presidents, but has not yet chosen a woman as its chief executive officer.

Meanwhile, women wonder about the hierarchical style of leadership in the first place and whether some other more egalitarian, less competitive arrangement of leadership might someday emerge. Yale professor of theology Letty Russell has

Barbara Brown Zikmund is director of the Hartford Theological Center, Hartford, Connecticut. This article is excerpted from "Ministry of Word and Sacrament: Women and Changing Understandings of Ordination," in *The Presbyterian Predicament: Six Perspectives*, ed. Milton J. Coalter, John M. Mulder, Louis B. Weeks (Louisville: Westminster/John Knox Press, 1990), 143, 148–58, 177–79.

written of a roundtable approach both to leadership within communions and to ecumenical leadership in the search for Christian unity.[1] Such ideas need further discussion and development, but they are signs, along with many others, that leadership, authority and power are being tested in new and hopeful ways throughout the church.

Barbara Brown Zikmund's article speaks not only to the issue of women and ordination, but also to the issue of women and leadership in general. In the final analysis, women's claim to ordination may be a claim to challenge the church's concept of ministry, leadership, power and authority in all its manifestations.

A reflection on the ordination of the first woman bishop in the Anglican Communion, p. 81, illustrates the tensions as well as the joys such appointments represent for women.

SC

◇

Tensions and ambiguities surrounding ordination have been in the Christian church for centuries. In the last hundred and fifty years, however, women have further complicated the situation. Christian women have come to the conclusion that they have a personal calling *to* and a talent *for* ordained ministry. Although many ecclesiastical authorities and traditions have not agreed that women can or should serve as ordained ministers or priests, more and more women have sought ordination. The desire of women to be ordained has aggravated longstanding tensions around ordination.

The statistics are well known, but let us review what has happened. In 1853 a small Congregational church in South Butler, New York, ordained Antoinette Brown to the Christian ministry. This is generally recognized as the first ordination of a woman in a major Christian ecclesiastical tradition. Other American women in Unitarian, Universalist, Northern Baptist and Disciples churches sought and gained ordination in the latter half of the nineteenth century. However, at the beginning of the twentieth century less than one half of one percent of all clergy in America were women. Most of these women were outside the Reformed tradition, serving Pentecostal, holiness or paramilitary groups like the Salvation Army. After a long

---

1. See Letty M. Russell, "Searching for a Roundtable in Church and World," in Melanie A. May, ed., *Women and the Church: The Challenge of Ecumenical Solidarity in an Age of Alienation* (Grand Rapids: Wm. B. Eerdmans; New York: Friendship Press, 1991), 163ff.

and complex struggle, in the 1950s the Methodists and several Presbyterian groups voted to ordain women to ministries of Word and sacrament. It took another fifteen to twenty years before major Lutheran denominations and the Episcopalians approved the ordination of women. Roman Catholic women are still seeking admission to the priesthood.[2]

. . .

Since the early 1970s the enrollment of women in theological seminaries has dramatically increased — women were under 5 percent in 1972 preordination programs; they were 22 percent in 1988. The shift is even more dramatic when we compare the number of male and female seminary graduates earning the Master of Divinity degree during the last decade. In 1977, 462 women graduated (8.4 percent), whereas in 1987, 1,496 women graduated (21.4 percent). This increase in the number of female M.Div. graduates (224 percent) contrasts sharply with the fact that during the same period of time the number of male seminary graduates increased very little (4.6 percent). In 1987, 33.5 percent of all Presbyterian seminary graduates were women.... Women were 38.1 percent of United Methodist graduates, 30.4 percent of Disciples, 29.8 percent of American Baptists, 36.4 percent of Episcopalians and 47.6 percent of United Church of Christ graduates. Not all women who graduate from seminary seek ordination, but many of them do.[3]

In my research on women and ordination I have been examining the efforts of women to gain ordination in mainline Protestant de-

---

2. Constant H. Jacquet, Jr., *Women Ministers in 1977* (New York National Council of Churches, 1978). For a more detailed description of the movement of women into ordination in mainline Protestantism see Barbara Brown Zikmund, "The Struggle for the Right to Preach," in Rosemary Radford Ruether and Rosemary Skinner Keller, eds., *Women and Religion in America*, vol. 1: *The Nineteenth Century* (San Francisco: Harper & Row, 1981), 191–241; and "Winning Ordination in Mainstream Protestantism: 1900–1965," in Rosemary Radford Ruether and Rosemary Skinner Keller, eds., *Women and Religion in America*, vol. 3: *The Twentieth Century* (San Francisco: Harper & Row, 1985), 339–83. [For a perspective on the Orthodox Church in regard to masculine and feminine participation and leadership, see Susannah Herzel, "The Orthodox," in *A Voice for Women* (Geneva: World Council of Churches, 1981), 142–48. —Ed.]

3. William Baumgaertner, ed., *Fact Book on Theological Education 1987–88* (Vandalia, Ohio: Association of Theological Schools in the United States and Canada, 1988). [By 1990, in most of these denominations, the percentage of women *enrolled* in seminaries had increased by approximately another 4 percent from 1987 percentages. The United Methodist Church, according to its Division of Ordained Ministry, had reached 42.8 percent enrollment in 1990 from 40.9 percent in 1988 and 42.3 percent in 1989. "The past two years may signify a "leveling off" of the percentage of women in U.M. Seminaries," the report concluded. —Ed.]

WOMEN CLERGY IN CANADIAN CHURCHES

The pattern for seminary education and consequent ordination in the churches of Canada has been quite similar to that of churches in the United States. Predecessor churches of the United Church of Canada approved ordination of women in 1934, and the first ordination of a woman to ministry occurred in 1936. By 1988 the number of women seminary graduates in the United Church of Canada and the Anglican and Presbyterian denominations ranged from 40 to 43 percent of the total graduates. In the Baptist tradition, by 1988 approximately 33 percent of the total seminary graduates were women. Not all women who graduate from seminary become ordained to the ministry of word and sacrament, of course, but more and more the trend in both the United States and Canada is toward a more equitable representation of women among those theologically trained for ministry.

nominations, but I have also sought to understand the experience of ordination from women's perspective. How do women appropriate the meaning of ordination and make it their own?

The Woman's Perspective

Let me speak autobiographically to set the stage. I grew up in a Congregational church in the 1950s. Active in the youth program of that large church in Detroit, Michigan, during high school, I decided that I was going to be a minister. I loved the church and, to be honest, I also loved (or had a teenage crush on) the young associate minister. I had never seen a woman minister, but I wanted to be one. I wanted to continue the sense of excitement, meaning and community that I found in my church. I was not out to prove anything. I certainly was not a feminist. I was simply a young girl with a desire to share my experience of God and church with others. There was no dramatic call or decisive moment. I found myself naturally growing toward a vocational role in church service.

To make a long story short, during my senior year in high school I "went in care" as a candidate for the "Christian ministry"; and

seven years later, after four years of college and three years of
seminary, I returned to Mayflower Congregational Church to be ordained. That was twenty-five years ago, in 1964. What did I think
I was doing? I realize now that I was not very self-conscious about
ordination. It was a ritual and a status that celebrated my love af-
fair with the church, but I did not bother a great deal about its
historical, theological or ecumenical meaning. By that time I was
married to a man who planned to be a college professor and so I
pragmatically decided that I would be a campus minister. As the
1960s flowed into the 1970s the question of women's ordination
became more visible and I became more reflective. I watched the
difficulties surrounding ordination for Episcopal women. I read a
great deal in the literature of the women's liberation movement. I
began to see how women were challenging some of the unexam-
ined assumptions about ordination. I began to meet women who
had struggled against prejudice and hostility to become ordained,
only to find that it was an ambiguous victory. Ordination carries so
many patriarchal assumptions that women find themselves increasingly ambivalent about its value. As one woman put it, "When I
was not ordained I thought I needed its recognition and authority,
but now that I've got it, I question any ecclesiology or theology of
ministry that needs it." For many women today the vocational crisis is not whether the church will ordain them but whether they
want to be ordained. The critique women bring to ordination relates to many of the issues embedded in my earlier discussion of
the history of ordination. Three areas of tension are worth exploring
more specifically.

Local or Universal?

First, there has been an ongoing tension between ordination as local
and ordination as universal. In the earliest eras of church history,
ordination (the specific setting apart of some persons by prayer and
laying on of hands) was to empower local leaders *and* to enable
evangelistic witness beyond the local setting. Initially, local clergy
were connected to the community, and the people insisted that eu-
charistic acts should not be conducted without clergy present; later,
the argument was reversed and the Eucharist became invalid unless
ordained leaders presided.

Women today are questioning all objective and universal definitions of ordination. They have noted the self-contradiction and
incoherence of theologies of priesthood and ministry that "twist the

ON THIS DAY

Although the day was crisp and cold, the sun was shining as I boarded the Pan Am shuttle to Boston. I was on my way to join eight thousand other witnesses to the historic ordination of Barbara Clementine Harris as the first woman bishop in the Anglican Communion. I felt both anticipation and sadness as I boarded the shuttle. I anticipated the consecration, the first ordination of a woman bishop in the 450 years of Anglican tradition and an altogether unprecedented event in the two-thousand-year history of the church catholic. But I was also sad because I sensed that this victory was not won without pain, anger, rancor and bitterness, and that the struggle was not over. The Boston setting bespoke the truth of my sense of sadness. As Harvey Cox put it when commenting on the ordination:

Boston has never been particularly friendly to women preachers.... Within a decade of its founding the Puritan divines drove Anne Hutchinson out of the colony for organizing a religious discussion group in her parlor — "not a fitting activity for women," they decreed. Then a few decades later the same serious gentlemen publicly hanged Mary Dyer, a Quaker, on the Common. The alleged witches of nearby Salem fared no less badly. So for a city where history always weighs heavy on the present, the consecration of Barbara Clementine Harris as Suffragan Bishop in the nation's largest Episcopal diocese did not go unnoticed either by the living or the dead. (Christianity and Crisis [March 20, 1989], 78)

There is no doubt that there are those who will leave the Episcopal Church because of this historic event. But in Boston on the day of Barbara Harris's ordination, their voices were muted. On this day, the Episcopal Church in the United States witnessed to the watching world that it is a church in solidarity with women.

— Joan Brown Campbell, a minister of the Christian Church (Disciples of Christ), is General Secretary of the National Council of Churches of Christ. An excerpt from her essay in Melanie A. May, ed., *Women and the Church: The Challenge of Ecumenical Solidarity in an Age of Alienation* (Grand Rapids: Wm. B. Eerdmans; New York: Friendship Press, 1991), 77, 78 humility of Christ into a religion of power."[4] They have come to the conclusion that the issue is not whether women can become priests or bishops; the issue is the "transformation of our religious institutions." How can women (and men) "convert Christianity to the gender-free faith which they are certain Jesus intended?" *Newsweek* magazine has noted that putting women in the pulpit is no longer the prime goal of Christian feminists. Rather, the aim is a "thorough comprehensive transformation of the language, symbols, and sacred texts of the Christian faith."[5] Ordination is seriously questioned because, as one Episcopal radical feminist writes, "ordination *in itself* does not bestow the least spiritual authority, personal holiness, specialized knowledge of ways into God or privileged access to God. Neither does ordination bestow prerogatives of coercive power."[6]

Women clergy in particular find that the "set apart" traditions of ordination perpetuate patterns of hierarchy that are increasingly dysfunctional in mainline white churches. Women choose to reject ontological definitions of "absolute consecration," and women also are moving beyond viewing ordination as merely personal choice or local service.

The work of contemporary scholars in the psychology field suggests some new ways to think about ordination that transcend both ontological and functional perspectives. Jean Baker Miller, author of *Toward a New Psychology of Women*, notes that women are seeking autonomy, but they want something more complete than "autonomy as men have defined it." Women want deeper relationships and holistic selfhood at the same time. It seems to me that many of the recent insights from the new psychology of women found in the writings of Mary Field Belenky, Blythe McVicker Clinchy, Nancy Rule Goldberger, Jill Mattuck Tarule, Nancy Chodorow and Carol Gilligan describe how women may be appropriating and transforming historic definitions of ordination.[7]

If women thrive on relationships and the fullness of life comes

---

4. Maggie Ross, *Pillars of Flame: Power, Priesthood, and Spiritual Maturity* (San Francisco: Harper & Row, 1988), 5.

5. Kenneth L. Woodward, "Feminism and the Churches," *Newsweek* (February 13, 1989), 58–61.

6. Maggie Ross, *Pillars of Flame*, 28.

7. See Jean Baker Miller, *Toward a New Psychology of Women* (Boston: Beacon Press, 1976); Nancy Chodorow, *The Reproduction of Mothering* (Berkeley, Calif.: University of California Press, 1978); and Carol Gilligan, *In a Different Voice: Psychological Theory and Women's Development* (Cambridge, Mass.: Harvard University Press, 1982). See also Mary Field Belenky, Blythe McVicker Clinchy, Nancy Rule Goldberger and Jill Mattuck Tarule, *Women's Ways of Knowing: The Development of Self, Voice and Mind* (New York: Basic Books, 1986).

when they can weave themselves into a web of strong relationships that are empowering, activating, honest and close, then ordained women will define the function and the status of ordained ministry differently. This is consistent with recent work in women's psychology that describes patterns of "mutual empathy" or "intersubjectivity." Standard developmental psychology (as well as predominant understandings of calling to ordination) tends to stress development as a process of individuation, independence and autonomy. These characteristics are the marks of psychological maturity (and of spiritual discernment). Yet when women are measured by such standards they are considered relatively immature and dependent. Carol Gilligan's book *In a Different Voice* and Mary Belenky's (and others') study of epistemology in *Women's Ways of Knowing* argue that men make moral decisions by thinking about rights while most women make moral choices by thinking and feeling about webs of responsibilities within relationships.[8]

For women, "relationality" is basic, yet the entire culture devalues relationships while expecting women to specialize in them. We should not be surprised, therefore, that ordination for women produces the same double bind. To be set apart by prayer and laying on of hands is an isolating communal act. Women need to keep relationality and enlarge the relational context, rather than focus upon separation and exclusivity.[9]

Lynn Rhodes, interviewing clergywomen for her book *Co-Creating: A Feminist Vision of Ministry*, found that clergywomen did not tie their sense of vocation to being ordained. In the context of community, clergywomen know that ordination does influence the way they are perceived and they cherish the gifts they receive because they are ordained. However, Rhodes writes, for them the issue is not to deny the value of such relationships, or the power they have, but to extend the possibility that other people of the community can also be seen as trustworthy and as having resources and strength for one another in times of crisis. In that sense, the clergyperson is not any more a "representative" than anyone else who identifies with the community. The issue, as one woman put it, is how "we all model with and for each other the meaning of our lives."[10]

---

8. See *Women's Ways of Knowing*, ibid.

9. Christina Robb, "A Theory of Empathy," *Boston Globe Magazine* (October 16, 1988), 18–19, 42ff.

10. Lynn Rhodes, *Co-Creating: A Feminist Vision of Ministry* (Philadelphia: Westminster Press, 1987), 114.

A United Church of Christ pastor shared with me her vision of ordained ministry as leadership for the upbuilding of the faithful *community.* It is not just being pastoral to individuals. The ordained one is literally called to "cure the soul of the church," to provide vision, to show the way during a time of declining expectations.

Like many women clergy, this pastor is especially concerned about the marginalization of the laity. Unfortunately, she notes, local and wider church life is all structured to pull people in and to build up the institutional church. This is backward. The church is the body Christ gathered for worship *and* scattered over the face of the earth as disciples and ministers of Jesus Christ. All are baptized to an outreach ministry, and the ordained clergy exist to "equip the saints for the work of ministry" (Eph. 4:13–16).

This pastor insists, therefore, that the ordained are not the "set apart" ones. At baptism every Christian has been set apart. Whereas at ordination some are set "in the midst of" those who are set apart — set in the midst to serve and equip the church for ministry. She concludes, "As a Christian I do participate in the 'power of the sacred,' but no more so than any other person who is self-consciously 'in Christ.'"[11]

From the earliest decades of the church, the tensions between the local and wider church, between personal salvation and institutional nurture, between individual integrity and relational needs and between laity and clergy have shaped understandings of ordination. Women bring significant insights to these concerns in our times.

Word or Sacrament?

Second, there has been an ongoing tension over whether ordination has more to do with ministries of the Word or ministries at the sacramental table. In the earliest era, almost all scholars agree, acts of "ordination" had nothing to do with sacraments; ordination authorized preaching and teaching. Over the centuries, however, ordination has increasingly been connected with sacramental leadership. Although the general Protestant insistence that ordination is not a sacrament and the Reformed traditions around the ordination of ruling elders have tempered this trend, ecumenical developments have emphasized that ordination is to priestly leadership at the Eucharist, or Lord's Supper.

---

11. Davida Foy Crabtree, "Empowering the Ministry of the Laity in Workplace, Home and Community: A Programmatic and Systemic Approach in the Local Church," doctor of ministry project, Hartford Theological Seminary, 1988, 98.

This is very interesting. In the development of American Protestantism there has been a great deal of latitude about the relationship of ordination to preaching. Schoolteachers and other learned leaders in the Reformed tradition preached in many colonial pulpits, but they refused to preside over the Lord's Supper. Why? Given our Reformed theology it ought to be the other way around. Methodism licensed local preachers but allowed only ordained elders to administer the sacrament without restrictions. Early on, women evangelists and lecturers were allowed to preach and teach, but when they sought ordination there was a problem. Why?

In the modern post-Enlightenment era, some of the ambiguity about ordination relates to our understanding of professions and recent efforts to define ministry as a profession. William F. May, of Southern Methodist University, suggests that there are tensions between a Christian vocation, a profession and a career. Every Christian has a vocation, which as traditionally conceived involves a commitment to God and neighbor. A career, however, is a more selfish thing; it is a means to pursue one's own private aims and purposes. Instead of asking what is the need of the community, a career orientation asks what do *I* want to be? Where do *I* want to go?[12]

The professional, and we like to think of ministry as a profession, stands somewhere between the vocation and the career. Originally the word "profess" meant literally "to testify on behalf of," or "to stand for something." For this reason being a "professional" carries implications about knowledge and moral responsibility. The professional knows something that will benefit the wider community, and he or she has a responsibility to use that knowledge to serve the wider human community. Yet professional services always involve an uneven interaction between the professional and the client. For this reason, as May puts it, a healthy professional exchange requires that the professional be "sufficiently distanced from his/her own interests and convenience to serve the client's own well-being."[13]

Good professionals also know more than others about some things. There is an elitism built into all professional work. Professionals have information that average ordinary people do not have. And they develop what May calls "cognitive superiority which spills

---

12. William F. May, "Vocation, Career, and Profession," paper presented at "To Serve the Present Age," Consultation on Evangelicals and American Public Life, sponsored by the Institute for the Study of American Evangelicals, November 17–19, 1988, typescript, 3, 6.

13. Ibid., 10–15.

over into a form of moral disdain for the client." In response the professional relationship cultivates a passivity in those who are not "in the know."[14]

It is not surprising, therefore, that for many women a heavy emphasis on the ordained ministry as a "profession" creates a problem. Women, who have often been clients, or even victims, in professional relationships are especially sensitive to the uneven power dynamics of ordination in the church. If the emphasis is on the ministry of the Word, there are dangers of intellectual elitism that keep laity passive and clergy in control. If the emphasis is on a more sacramental ministry, there are dangers of institutional isolation from ministry in the world.

One way out of the elitism implicit in ordination to ministries of the Word is to recapture the importance of teaching as well as preaching. Preaching seeks transformation. But transformational leadership in all professions runs the danger of paternalism. As May notes, "The professional who insists on transforming the client's behavior, but who neglects to teach the client inevitably relies on managerial, manipulative and condescending modes of behavior control."[15] This is something women know all too well.

When ministry focuses on teaching rather than preaching, however, the professional relationship is different. The act of teaching engages the other with respect. It treats the other as a whole human self and builds up the church for service in the world. Teaching, not preaching, should stand at the core of authentic ministry.

Another way out of the isolation and irresponsibility sometimes found in ordination to sacramental ministries is to shift the sacramental focus. Protestantism upholds two biblically based sacraments — baptism and the Eucharist (or Lord's Supper or Communion). Most discussions about ordination and the sacraments revolve around the Table — not around baptism.

But what would happen if the sacramental center of the church and its major ecclesiastical energy was focused on baptism rather than Communion? Women have suggested that some of their difficulty with ordained sacramental leadership would be changed by such an emphasis. We are all called to ministry through our baptism. There is neither lay nor ordained, there is neither male nor female, all are equal in the Spirit through baptism.

If ministry of the Word was viewed as a ministry of teaching

---

14. Ibid., 18–19.
15. Ibid., 25–26 (emphasis added).

and preaching, and if the ministry of sacraments focused on baptism rather than the Table, ordination would carry a very different meaning. Theologically we say that laity and ordained persons are called to exercise differing forms of the one ministry of Christ which is shared by the whole people of God. Recent ecumenical theology begins with this basic truth but continues to insist on the historic orders of bishop, presbyter and deacon. Traditions around those orders for women are not helpful.

It is not surprising, therefore, that ordained women are very wary that a theology of ministry grounded in the priesthood of all believers will still be subverted. As the COCU Consensus puts it, "Lay status in the Church is not a residual status, but rather the primary form of ministry apart from which no other Christian ministry can be described." Laity must never be defined as the ones who are "not ordained" or "not professional." Clergy and laity have Christian vocations each with special responsibilities.[16]

From the earliest decades of the church the tensions between Word and sacrament, between teaching and preaching, between baptism and the Lord's Supper, between laity and clergy have shaped understandings of ordination. Women bring significant insights into these concerns in our times.

Office and Person

Finally, there has been an ongoing tension around the relationship between the office and the person of the ordained minister. This is because the ordination of women calls for renewed recognition of the power of sexuality in human community, especially in the church. In a professional ethics research group that I am part of in Berkeley, California, we have surveyed male and female clergy on questions of sexual ethics and issues of homosexuality, ordination and ministry.

Women, especially clergywomen, insist that an ethic of sexual behavior cannot be divorced from issues of power and from affirmations of sexuality as part of God's good creation. Yet in Western society, women have always been associated with the "lower" or "lesser" forces that perpetuate the struggles between culture and nature or between spirit and flesh. As such, women often see power from the underside, and therefore women clergy feel that they are able to relate to powerlessness more effectively.

---

16. *The COCU Consensus: In Quest of a Church of Christ Uniting* (Princeton, N.J.: Consultation on Church Union, 1985), para. 25 (emphasis added).

Simply being an ordained woman challenges the cultural habit of separating sexuality and spirituality. Because she is a woman in a culture that does not value women, an ordained woman must come to terms with her sexuality in ways that male clergy can avoid. Women clergy must affirm the goodness of sexuality in the process of affirming themselves.

Ordained women ministers also remind us of the connection between sexuality and power. As ordained persons they hold the power of position; as women they find their power denied or usurped. When we asked ordained women about sexual ethical dilemmas in their work, we found that women are much more concerned with defending themselves than they are worried about the power or danger of their own sexual improprieties. The larger culture assumes that women will set the boundaries in sexual encounters, and clergywomen continue to carry that responsibility.[17]

. . .

From the earliest decades of the church, tensions between body and spirit, between the carnal and the holy, and between power and weakness have shaped understandings of ordination. Women bring significant insights into these concerns in our times.

The Reformed tradition has made strong contributions to the theology and practice of ministry since the sixteenth century. In its willingness to retrieve the importance of the priesthood of all believers and in its decisions to ordain women to ministries of Word and sacrament, it has challenged and will continue to enrich our understanding of some of the long-standing tensions around the practice of ordination. Women in ministry:

- Question all universal, indelible, power-focused understandings of ordination

- Identify with theories of women's psychology that uphold autonomy without sacrificing relationality

- Seek to extend ministry beyond institutional maintenance

- View themselves as "set in the midst" of the faithful community rather than "set apart"

- Are wary of professional definitions of ministry that rely on patterns of elitism and dependency

---

17. A summary of the Professional Ethics Group findings was prepared by Maura Tucker, "Women in Ministry: Sexual Ethics," typescript available from the Center for Ethics and Social Policy, Graduate Theological Union, Berkeley, Calif., 1988.

- Affirm the importance of teaching, which transforms without patronizing
- Celebrate the sacrament of baptism, which ordains all Christians to ministry
- Reject understandings of laity as "nonclergy" or "nonprofessional"
- Refuse to separate sexuality, spirituality and power
- Recognize that character and ethical standards are part of Christian discipleship.

Many men do these same things, but I am convinced that as more and more women attend seminary and confront the question of ordination, our definitions and practices related to ordination will change. It is not yet clear exactly what will happen, but something is happening.

◊ **9** ◊

The Mind-Body Split

JOY BUSSERT

In the essay that follows, Joy Bussert explores the implications of excessive male control of women, which the author demonstrates was the result of a distorted theology. The purpose of including this depressing chapter is not to chastise contemporary men to whom such practices are as abhorrent as they are to women, but rather to remind us that even though such theological thinking about mind and body is now rejected or modified, it is still operative in too many pockets of our society, justifying blatant abuse of women.

Furthermore, it is as if the legacy of associating woman's body with sin has been programmed into our very genes — a sort of collective memory — still determining our basic responses (both male and female) far more than we would like to acknowledge.[1]

Joy Bussert writes that her book "comes out of her work with the shelters for battered women in Minnesota," and at the end of this selection describes the church's role in offering space where truth can be told.   *SC*

Joy Bussert, a minister in the Evangelical Lutheran Church in America, is completing her doctorate at Union Theological Seminary in New York. This article is adapted from her book *Battered Women: From a Theology of Suffering to an Ethic of Empowerment* (Minneapolis: Augsburg-Fortress, 1986), 5–15, 17–18, 78–79.

1. For an extensive description of how this played itself out in nineteenth-century America, especially among the male clergy, see Matilda Joslyn Gage, *Woman, Church and State: The Original Exposé of Male Collaboration against the Female Sex* (1893), introduction by Sally Roesch Wagner, foreword by Mary Daly (Watertown, Mass.: Persephone Press, 1980).

◇

Our own theological church, as we know it, has scorned and vilified the body till it has seemed almost a reproach to have one, yet at the same time has credited it with the power to drag the soul to perdition.

— Eliza Farnham, nineteenth-century writer

We MUST BEGIN with the church's historic devaluation of the body in order to understand fully the social problem of violence against women. Rooted in the ancient philosophical split between the spirit and matter, this devaluation of the body permeates Christian thought from the early church fathers up through the theological thinkers of our own day. Theologically, this pessimistic view of the body fostered an antisexuality bias that not only included a bias against women, but ultimately provided churchly sanction for violence against them.

This bias found its most blatant expression in the mind-body dualism of classical Greek philosophy and culture as it emerged at the beginning of the Christian era. The religious transformation in the Greek world from the Apollonian celebration of the body to the Platonic escape from the body radically changed the direction of Western thought and set the philosophical context for Western Christianity.

This bias against the body is evident in Plato's dialogue, the *Phaedo*, for example, where Plato speaks of the man who pursues truth through "pure and unadulterated thought" by cutting himself off from all of his senses and his body, which Plato argues "is an impediment preventing the soul from attaining to truth and clear thinking. . . . "

. . .

Of course, we must acknowledge at the outset that there have been alternatives to mind-body dualism within the Judeo-Christian tradition. Although early Hebrew life and culture, for example, were clearly male dominated, they did exhibit very real affirmations of the body, of sexuality and of marriage as good gifts from God. However, the cultural environment in which early Christianity found itself included other powerful influences that were to shape the thinking of the early communicators of the Christian faith. Thus, despite the Christian emphasis on the goodness of creation and the wholeness of the human person in the unity of mind and body that is clearly evident in the teachings of St. Paul, Plato's dualistic spirituality crept into the thinking of the church's early theologians at a number of different levels.

First, the church fathers incorporated this "ethic of alienation from the body" into their theological system by making the rejection of the body and the flight of the soul from the material, sensual nature a prerequisite for redemption. Since the soul — or spirit — was thought to be imprisoned in an inferior sensual nature, the goal of salvation was to free the pure soul from the evil material body. In the words of the fourth-century theologian Jerome: "You must act against nature or rather above nature...and while in the body to live as though out of it."

The application of this body-denying ethic by the church fathers to their experience as men in relation to women was the second step in the appropriation of Platonic spirituality into Christian thought.... The early church fathers, from a Christian standpoint, could not speak of two creations, one spiritual and good, the other material and evil. Women thus entered the picture as convenient scapegoats in the church fathers' attempt to resolve a prior theological problem. Since the soul's flight from the body was a precondition for salvation, the body, they concluded, must be the source of human sin. And since it was woman who presented them, as men, with a "body" problem, they further concluded that sexuality — specifically female sexuality — was responsible for the Fall of creation.

. . .

Throughout the Middle Ages, this association of women with the body...and the consequent fear of female sexuality, continued to color the male perception of women. Although marriage was deemed necessary, celibacy was elevated to a higher and holier calling by many Christian thinkers.

Although affirming marriage and family life, the Protestant Reformation did not break entirely with the dualistic spirituality of medieval religious thought. Luther still maintained a rather negative posture toward sexuality and treated women as a shameful necessity for the outlet of "uncontrollable" human impulses....

Sexuality appears to be what men most feared in themselves. The higher principles, mind and spirit, were labeled "male," and the lower principles, body and matter, were labeled "female." Man represented mind; woman represented body. Man had the capacity for reason and intellect; woman the capacity for emotion and feeling.

This dualistic view of the self, the world, of man as mind and woman as the alien "sexual other" shaped Western consciousness and reinforced the age-old principle of hierarchy as the appropriate

pattern for human relationships.... As men assumed for themselves
the superior capacities of rationality and spirituality and assigned to
women the capacities of emotionality and sensuality, men were naturally to take precedence in church, domestic and public life. And
since femaleness was equated with the inferior body, it followed that
woman must naturally live in submission to man... even as the body
must be subject to the spirit, in the right ordering of the Christian
life.

Image of God

This patterning of the "spiritual male mind" over the "carnal female
body" held several serious theological repercussions for women.
First, because of her status as the lesser half of the mind-body dichotomy, religious thinkers through the ages denied that woman was
created in the image of God.

Historically, theological discussions about the human person have
revolved around the doctrine of the *Imago Dei*. In its purest form this
doctrine states that our worth and dignity as persons are grounded
in the conviction that we are created in the image of God. However, theologians have consistently denied women the capacity to be
bearers of the *Imago Dei*, and thus ignored their inherent worth as
persons created in the image of God.

Augustine, for example, drawing on the familiar metaphor from
Ephesians 5:23, interprets Paul to mean that the woman has no head
of her own, but that her husband is her head as she is his body, and
thus defines the male alone as the one created in the full image of
God.

. . .

Although the Reformers expressed a greater appreciation for the
female sex, she still could not equal the man as far as the image of
God was concerned. Speaking of Eve, Luther insisted that "although
she was a most extraordinary creature similar to Adam as far as the
image of God is concerned, she was nevertheless a woman...."

The woman, according to Luther, is not only deficient in her capacity to image God; because of the Fall, she must also accept her
assigned subordinate role in life. Any unwillingness or effort on her
part to change it represents a stubborn revolt against her rightful
place as a "domestic creature" in relation to man.

. . .

The situation is not much better for women in Calvin's scheme
of things. Although he placed special emphasis on compatibility in

marriage, the arrangement was clearly hierarchical, not egalitarian. Marital stability still depended on the woman's submission to her husband in all things. As with Luther, any woman who challenged this male authority was sinful, rebellious and disruptive of the God-given pattern for family relationships. This bias appears in Calvin's reply to a woman who wrote to him seeking refuge from an abusive husband:

> We have a special sympathy for women who are evilly and roughly treated by their husbands, because of the roughness and cruelty of the tyranny and captivity which is their lot. We do not find ourselves permitted by the Word of God, however, to advise a woman to leave her husband, except by force of necessity; and we do not understand this force to be operative when a husband behaves roughly and uses threats to his wife, not even when he beats her, but only when there is imminent peril to her life, whether from persecution by the husband or by his conspiring.... We exhort her to bear with patience the cross which God has seen fit to place upon her; and mean-while not to deviate from the duty which she has before God to please her husband, but to be faithful whatever happens.[2]

The Right of Chastisement

This leads us to the second theological repercussion for woman from the patterning of the pure male mind over the carnal female body. The perception of woman as loathsome body responsible for sin and as submissive body in the ordering of human relationships not only gave social sanction to her status as dutiful subordinate wife, but also granted her husband the right to "correct" or "chastise" her as the erring evil body. This "power of correction" or "right of chas-tisement," as it was called, gave religious and legal sanction for the absolute control of the "male mind" over the "female body" in the form of physical violence.

. . .

Thus the philosophical assumptions behind Platonic spirituality put women at a decided disadvantage in civil and ecclesiastical

2. [Calvin's reply to his parishioner is virtually identical with the advice a con-temporary woman reports receiving from her minister: "Early in our marriage I went to a clergyman who, after a few visits, told me that my husband meant no real harm, that he was just confused and felt insecure. I was encouraged to be more tolerant and understanding. Most important, I was told to forgive him the beatings just as Christ had forgiven me from the cross." Cited in Dell Martin, *Battered Wives*, rev. ed. (Volcano, Calif.: Volcano Press, 1981), 2. —Ed.]

law and even condoned and encouraged violence against them.
...But what about the corresponding deficiency in the male? If
women were the historic sustainers of the body half of the mind-
body spirit, that is, if they were the ones destined to embody the
human capacities for emotion and sensuality, where did that leave
men?

Although the theologians and thinkers of our Christian past
preached at length on woman's deficiency and flaunted their own
superiority as rational, spiritual beings,...they were, in fact, de-
priving themselves of one-half of what it means to be a whole,
integrated human person. As the historic sustainers of the mind half
of the mind-body dichotomy, men were thus deprived of all that
is associated with the body, including the capacity for emotion and
sensuality. Men were asked to live with an inner alienation that
not only shaped their individual and collective self-understanding,
but also their conception of what it means to be in relationship
to others.

Sin, in Christian thought, has often been defined as alienation
from self, God and others. Clearly this definition fits well for our
discussion of violence against women. For what greater alienation
is there than to cut oneself off from what it means to be a whole
human person and to project that inner division onto others through
self-elevation and even violence?

What we have not begun to deal with in the church is the notion
of alienation from one's total self and from the body as a manifestation of human sin, and how that alienation and deficiency have
been projected onto women in patriarchal thinking.

This, then, is precisely the heart of the matter: projected fear
and hatred directed at women as the fallen "inferior" bodily half
of the mind-body dichotomy, and male "superiority" and alienation
from their own bodily selves are the root causes of violence directed
against women.

Men today who come into the treatment programs for violent
partners are men who suffer from the culturally imposed mind-body
split within themselves and who choose to project it outward onto
women through physical violence. They are products of the verbal
violence contained in the writings of the religious thinkers of our
inherited past. This verbal violence, as we have seen, is rooted in
a profound sense of alienation from self, God and others and continues to foster hatred toward women and provide the theological
ammunition for violence against them.

We Must Begin to Question

Violence against women is a complex problem that involves more than just the brutal act itself or the personal interaction between any individual man or individual woman in marriage. Rather, when we speak of violence [toward women], we are addressing an ancient cultural flaw in our society that has been socially and historically conditioned and has its roots in the age-old attitudes toward women reflected in the institution of marriage, women's limited access to legal and economic leverage, and, as we have seen, religious dogma under a dominant male system.

It was not only the theologians of our past, however, who perpetuated the devaluation of women. The body-denying antiwoman ethic of Platonic spiritualism is also evident throughout history in the teachings of lawyers, philosophers, public officials and other secular leaders.

. . .

[Thus], the struggle on behalf of equality for women continues. Although the nineteenth and twentieth centuries have seen important legal reforms, . . . stubborn traces of attitudes that reveal a dominant male bias are still with us.

We must, therefore, begin to question the age-old sentiments that elevate the "spiritual male mind" over the "carnal female body." We must challenge the rhetoric of the Religious Right that seeks to preserve an outmoded notion of the hierarchical family, keeping women and men locked into a potentially violent cultural pattern and preventing the emergence of models for Christian relationships based on mutuality, reciprocity and wholeness. We must break down cultural sex-role stereotyping and make possible friendships between girls and boys, women and men, that are free of dualistic and hierarchical overtones and shaped according to the biblical concept of wholeness. Such an effort must envision not only theological reconstruction in our churches, but a world in which social and economic equality of the sexes becomes a reality.

This vision, of course, begins with our ability to risk, our willingness to share honestly and openly our feelings as women and men, as we struggle with this issue of violence. . . . The fact is that we are on a continuum. Women who are battered are living with the extreme manifestation of how all women are treated in this culture. And men who batter are simply taking what they have learned about being men in our culture and enforcing it violently. . . . To a greater or lesser degree, we are all victims of this suffocating cycle

VIOLENCE IN THE PARISHES

Thanks to groundbreaking work by the United Methodist Women in Crisis project, we now know that our local parishes include sizable number of victims of violence. But so far, church agencies and sociologists of religion have not been very interested in whether, or how many, victims turn to their clergy for support. Nor do we have anything beyond anecdotal evidence on how clergy treat abused women who do turn to them. Feminist grassroots groups may be wary of clergy because victims all too frequently report that their minister or priest exacerbated the victim's plight. ("This is a cross you must learn to bear" or "turn the other cheek" can be deadly dimensions of traditional Christian piety in this context.) Occasionally one does meet pastors who are aware, compassionate and active in coalition building for structural change, but we don't know how typical they are.

As increasing numbers of women enter seminaries, consciousness of such abuse has increased among ministers. This may be due to the unspoken solidarity among women since many of us will never be comfortable telling a man about these intimate wounds. It may be due to the fact that women in ministry are more aware of the threats and menaces against all women, and hence willing to speak about them, to communicate understanding and openness. It may also be a function of the sheer novelty of women in ministry: Because the bonds of congregational expectations are not yet solidified, new roles are possible for women clergy.

But women in ministry are few and far between, and over-extended. For change to occur, therefore, clergy men also must hear and respond in new ways....

Most essential is our communication at the local parish level, for that is where American churches and the Christian faith live and move and have their being.... There it is human interaction which is crucial. And it is there, I fear, that we most frequently fall short.

— Mary Pellauer, "Violence against Women: The Theological Dimension," *Christianity and Crisis* (May 30, 1983): 208, 209.

of violence. All of us, individually, must begin to address this issue within ourselves as we struggle for social transformation and work toward justice.... As the Reverend William Sloane Coffin so aptly states:

> From psychology and our own experience we have learned that the subconscious has no digestive tract. What goes down must come up again, and usually does so in the form of displaced violence. Those, for example, who repress in themselves their anger generally show more reverence for order than for life.... Men who repress in themselves the "feminine" side of their nature, will generally, in more or less subtle ways, be anti-feminine.... In short, there is an intimate relationship between inner and outer repression. Those who are themselves repressed become themselves repressive. This leads me to conclude that the woman most in need of liberation is the woman in every man. When at last this woman is liberated...along with the man in every woman...then, I think, our homes, the churches and the world, will be much better places. There can no longer be true community between women and men unless that community is based on full equality.[3]

. . .

Opening Prophetic Space

The following picture of four women who told their stories at a conference on battered women in rural Minnesota convinced me of the central role the church can and must play in opening the door of public silence about violence in the home.

It was the first and only workshop out of a program of twenty-six training conferences for clergy and lay leaders that was not held in a conference center or a Holiday Inn, but in the sanctuary of a rural church. As always, the anxiety level of the participants was intense as several battered women formed a panel in the middle of the chancel. A colorful stained-glass window shed light about them, lending a mystical quality to the picture.

As they told of their lives, I began to sense the significance of the scene before me. A simple wooden cross provided a backdrop for their words and became a symbol of both suffering and courage, of vulnerability and integrity. The light streaming through the open

---

3. From a speech delivered to the Eighth Annual Assembly of the World WMCA, Geneva, Switzerland, 1981.

door at the side of the chancel became a symbol of awakening and hope, of resurrection and new life.

I felt a certain transformation take place among the listeners as the women told of their stories — a movement from anxiety to quiet attentiveness, from curiosity to compassion. The notion of the church as a door opener for truth-telling itself emerged as a prophetic symbol for me as never before. These four women who had previously found refuge in a shelter, now opened the door and found sanctuary in a small country church, which became the prophetic space for them to tell their stories.

This experience reminded me that the church as sanctuary can no longer be only a refuge from fear, but must become a prophetic space in which to speak truth. Standing under the cross and in the light of the resurrection faith, we too, like these women, must be willing to speak the truth about violence in the home at all levels of our church's life and ministry. With them we must walk in faith through the thick locked door, breaking through the suffocating silence and the tragic darkness that hurts all of us.

◇ **10** ◇

All's Fair in Love and Work?

Occupational competition between men and women is complicated by the feelings of guilt aroused in the men, for aggression by males toward females assumes an emotional charge which is quite different from normal competition between men alone....In addition there is a practical consideration: for it may be predicted that sexual or quasi-sexual relationships of some importance will develop in most mixed working groups. Mixed groups in work pose an additional threat and disturb the carefully guarded separation between home and work which plays so large a part in the psychic economy of the modern bread-winner.

— Simone de Beauvoir, *The Second Sex*, 1953

This observation about men and women in daily working relationships is at the heart of the matter of appropriate ethics in the workplace. On the one hand we assume a kind of neutral partnership among men and women in a working atmosphere. On the other, we recognize that we are scarcely beyond the primitive mating instincts of the distant past when it comes to male/female behavior toward each other in *any* situation. The mating game is always in process in our psyches. And both men and women are often caught totally unprepared for dealing with it in constructive ways in the workplace.

Can we simply be good colleagues and co-workers — or even responsible competitors — expressing either a healthy attraction or a bristling polarity toward one another without letting loose destructive or undisciplined sex games that divert us from the task at hand, causing more social upheaval than we are capable of handling very well? This is a question not only in the settings where we earn our livelihoods, but in the settings for our volunteer and religious work, including the church.

Unfortunately, for too long we have depended upon our spiritual leaders, mostly men, to set the standards and define the boundaries for acceptable sexual behavior in social, religious and work environments, but in some instances, these leaders have become the worst offenders. We must now find new ways of being "priests to each other" about such matters.

Sociologists remind us that today we may very well meet more people in one week's time than our grandparents met in a lifetime, many of these in work-related situations. In such a fluid society, how do we manage both work and relationships, allowing for potentially deep and significant friendships in a common endeavor, while reserving for our primary relationships the intimacy and sexual bonding that belong to them?

This question has loomed large in importance as women enter the professional world as equals, not simply as the enablers of men's agendas. Neither men nor women will find the answers alone. Nor will we find the answers by simply ignoring the question. We need to put the issue on the church's agenda at every level and find ways of developing a social/work ethic that deals realistically and responsibly with collegiality and sexuality.

Certainly the increased media attention in recent months to sexual harassment has raised consciousness among men and women throughout this continent, if not the world. Those who have done major research in the field believe that in most cases sexual harassment in the workplace is not so much a botched flirtation as an assertion of power, a way of making the other person vulnerable so that her (or his) work will not have to be taken seriously.

Louise Fitzgerald, a psychologist at the University of Illinois, says that some harrassment simply results from a cultural lag. "Many men entered the workplace at a time when sexual teasing and innuendo were commonplace. They have no sense there's anything wrong with it," she says. "All they need is some education." But genuine harassers, Fitzgerald says, "continue to do offensive things even when a woman tells them it is obnoxious."[1]

Across the country churches are discovering that one of the more effective ways of approaching these issues is by means of seminars and workshops directed by highly skilled professional leaders in the fields of sociology and psychology as well as theology. Such seminars demand the commitment of both men and women to a process whereby they can discover together the difference between holistic, healthy affirmations of themselves as sexual beings and behavior that is destructive and inappropriate in the working environment.

---

1. Quoted in Daniel Goleman, "Sexual Harrassment: It's About Power, Not Lust," *New York Times*, October 22, 1991.

This kind of involved discussion is needed to interpret and also to help develop the policy statements on sexual harassment that many denominations are formulating at both national and regional levels.

Perhaps the time has come for the church to utilize the best professional help available in a search for a more mature, enlightened approach to sexuality in every arena of our lives.

SC

PART THREE

A Matter of Justice:
A Matter of Solidarity

◇

As we evaluate the women's movement and its effect on the life of the church, we need to be reminded of the role that the traditional women's missionary societies and their successor women's organizations have played in raising the consciousness of the church about matters of equality and justice. Many of the reforms that have come about in the churches' ways of working, worshiping and seeking justice are the direct result of processes set in motion over the years by church women's organizations. Chapter 11 describes this process in more detail.

The Ecumenical Decade itself is one result of this heightened consciousness about justice. When the World Council of Churches launched the decade in 1988, it identified these aims.

The Ecumenical Decade of the Churches in Solidarity with Women aims at:

1. Empowering women to challenge oppressive structures in the global community, their country and their church.

2. Affirming — through shared leadership and decision making, theology and spirituality — the decisive contributions of women in churches and communities.

3. Giving visibility to women's perspectives and actions in the work and struggle for justice, peace and the integrity of creation.

4. Enabling the churches to free themselves from racism, sexism and classism; from teachings and practices that discriminate against women.

5. Encouraging the churches to take actions in solidarity with women.

These goals are explored further in a statement of support for the decade drafted by the United Methodist Women's Division and later adopted as the denomination's official position on the decade. It stands as an example of how many communions are expressing visions of justice for and with women.

The contributions by Una Kroll of England and Aruna Gnanadason of India remind us that the decade is a worldwide observance and that women and men around the world are paying attention to the marginalization of women and to how the church should be responding.

SC

◇ **11** ◇

Beyond Co-optation: Women as Catalysts for Justice

Women's organizations within American Protestantism — originally organized as missionary societies — have gone several different directions in the second half of this century. But certainly one of their major roles has been that of raising the church's consciousness about women, and, in the process, about racism, sexism and classism. In fact, it was probably women who coined two of those terms.

"Sex" was a very private word in our culture, at least until the late 1930s. (If you were to peruse the popular magazines prior to that time, you wouldn't find the word mentioned.) Consequently, when women first began to talk about "sexism" in the church, it was perceived, even by most women, as a very unsettling subject. Classism was certainly something the church did not want to admit, but there it was, and again, it was women's organizations that surfaced the issue. Society at large was finally beginning to address racism, but in the church it was women's organizations that were in the vanguard of struggling with the problem of the *double* oppression of *women* of color.

In recent years, women's organizations have been in the forefront in surfacing issues of justice in relation to women. The list is long: women and poverty, particularly single female heads of households with children; women in prison, most for crimes related to money or means of getting money, such as prostitution; women and health care; women and survival after divorce; women's lack of access to political decisions affecting their lives; women and reproductive rights; abused women; women on drugs; women and work. So often, the issues are related to women's inability to have economic and social power in shaping their own lives and the lives of their children. Women's organizations have not shied away from the troublesome issues. In fact, they have usually taken the initiative in seeking systemic change.

In the Interest of Unity

However, women's organizations have continually been challenged to "join the church," to quit being a "shadow church" and to let their structures become a part of the whole. In the 1960s, in good faith, some women's organizations began to question continuing their separate structures. It was within the United Church of Christ tradition (among the Congregationalists of New England) that American women first began to organize for mission. Yet after more than a hundred years of impressive missionary activity the women's national organization within the UCC decided to give up its separate structure. The women disbanded at the national level, but instead of gaining more visibility and participation in the total mission of the church, they only lost a significant network of women who had been actively involved in the church's mission both nationally and internationally. Women of the Episcopal Church went through a similar experience in dismantling their women's organization. As a result, the women of both denominations later modified these positions, and each reconstructed a national network of women.

Others, like the Presbyterian Church U.S. (prior to the recent Presbyterian reunion), declared all women of the denomination as Women of the Church, maintaining structures for women's separate units at the local and regional level, as desired, but putting less emphasis on a separate national structure for women. The Lutheran, Baptist and other women's organizations struggled with how to affirm their readiness to be a part of the total church while working to guard against the kind of co-optation that the UCC and Episcopal women had experienced.

Elizabeth Howell Verdezi's *In but Still Out* is the story of how in the 1920s Presbyterian women gave over control of their mission boards in the interest of unity, only to be in the final analysis co-opted by the male agenda.[1] In theory and in fact, the women

---

1. Elizabeth Howell Verdezi, *In but Still Out* (Philadelphia: Westminster Press, 1973). In another case, Presbyterian women had gained the major positions in the church's task of Christian education. For their own professional status and advancement, they encouraged men to join in this effort as educators only to discover that once men had entered the picture, the higher salaries and the creative

were accorded representation on denominational boards established to replace their own separate boards, but in actuality any real power on the boards eluded them. Being a minority in a basically male structure and not privy to much of the information available to the primary male decision makers, they were at a decided disadvantage in any policy-making process.

Consciousness Must Be Raised

United Methodist Women, even during a number of mergers and reunions of their denomination, were the major group to continue their autonomy in a separate women's division of the denomination's General Board of Global Ministries, maintaining control of both their program and their funds. Two publications, *In the Middle of Tomorrow* by Barbara Campbell and *With Unveiled Face* by Theressa Hoover, tell a well-documented story of how United Methodist Women recognized both the needs and the power of women in mission and chose to maintain their structures to carry out their vision of the church's calling, particularly in regard to women and children.[2]

A United Methodist statement published in 1976 by the Women's Division stated: "We believe that the church is still in captivity to male values, structures and practices, and consequently is unable to be the locus of genuine community. We believe this to be true for all racial groups and in all countries. We must raise the reason for this captivity to the level of consciousness so that they may be examined, challenged and changed."[3]

The records of all the women's organizations tell a similar story. It is a story of more than half of the church's population functioning on the edge of the ecclesiastical structures while guarding innovative and creative programs to insure the development of women and to advocate the wholeness of the church.

Today, the women of most Protestant denominations in the U.S. and Canada (including the denominations of predominantly black membership) continue to maintain structures at national and regional levels to be "in mission" while they advocate women's rightful place in the total life of the church.

---

and decision-making national positions related to Christian education were going to the men.

2. Barbara Campbell, *In the Middle of Tomorrow* (2d ed., 1983), and Theressa Hoover, *With Unveiled Face* (1983) (New York: Women's Division, General Board of Global Ministries, United Methodist Church).

3. *Ministries to Women and Ministries to Children, Women's Division Policy Statement*, General Board of Global Ministries, United Methodist Church, 1976.

As the world church has provided opportunities to explore such issues as the ordination of women, inclusive language, the importance of feminist theological studies and feminist ethics, as well as issues of racism, sexism and classism, the support necessary to make such efforts possible most often has come from the women's organizations. Such support has included funding, the necessary networks established worldwide and innovative programming and planning.

The history of this period among women in American churches is yet to be written from an ecumenical point of view, but while women of all the denominations tell similar stories, they continue to seek a church that is in solidarity with them for the sake of a common mission.

The common mission, furthermore, seeks solidarity with all women. As has been pointed out, the marginalization of women in the church is directly related to the marginalization of women in all of society. An ultimate end of the church's mission is *justice*. For the church to be in solidarity with women, it must recognize its mission to seek justice for oppressed women everywhere.

SC

◇ **12** ◇

Away from the Margins

A STATEMENT OF
THE UNITED METHODIST CHURCH

This statement is excerpted from the resolution adopted by the
United Methodist Church in support of the Ecumenical Decade
of the Churches in Solidarity with Women, *The United Methodist Book of Resolutions*, 1988, 202–7. It is an excellent example
of the many resolutions presented by women to denominational policy-setting bodies at the beginning of the Decade of
the Churches in Solidarity with Women. This resolution origi-
nating in the United Methodist Women's Division became the
churchwide position on the decade.   *SC*

◇

WHEN WE LOOK AT WOMEN across the world we discover millions
who are still on the margin of their societies. Some are there largely
because they were born female instead of male. Others are on the
fringe because they are old in societies that want women to be
eternally young. Young women who are single parents with families have few marketable skills and cannot support their children.
Women may find themselves on the fringes of society because of
age, caste, class, color, ethnic or national origin or marital status.

The margin of society is dangerous. Women are forced to live
there by reason of poverty, famine, war, illiteracy, ageism, hand-
icapping conditions, refugee or illegal alien status, homelessness
or incarceration. Women are not the only ones to suffer. When
women suffer, there is a ripple effect. So central is the well-being
and economic security of a woman to the lives of others that her
marginalization adversely impacts not only the quality of her devel-

opment but that of her family and her community as a whole. The well-being of women is central to the well-being of all.

Signs of hope are emerging across the world as women are making the journey away from the fringes of society, empowering one another through care and struggle for life.

The United Nations Decade for Women (1975–1985) pointed the way to what can be done. Much is still before us.

The "Forward Looking Strategies for the Advancement of Women by the Year 2000" that emerged from the 1985 "End of the Decade" Conference (held in Nairobi, Kenya) should be implemented. The Ecumenical Decade of the Churches in Solidarity with Women builds on the momentum of the U.N. Decade for Women and gives the churches a new opportunity to respond to God's call for inclusiveness and solidarity and sharing of power. Some of the obstacles women face have been cited by the World Council of Churches as follows:

- In time of economic recession, women are among the first to be thrown out of work.

- Women in rural areas receive least attention in development plans and are not consulted about their basic needs.

- The effects of famine are hardest on women, who bear the heaviest responsibility for the family.

- As socio-economic situations deteriorate, frustration of jobless men often leads to increased sexual abuse and violence against women.

- Growing poverty, the spread of military bases and the promotion of sex-tourism have greatly increased the plague of prostitution, involving even younger women and children.

- Among the victims of nuclear testing are women, such as those in the Pacific, who bear the burden of increased miscarriages and deformed children.

- Women industrial workers are often without protection and receive the lowest wages from local and multinational industries, exploiting women's vulnerable positions.

- Apartheid and other forms of racism oppress women in a specific way and make them suffer often double and triple oppression as women, as poor and as racial/ethnic people.

These are all justice issues and men of the church and in society are joining women in acts of reformation, even re-creation, working to transform old orders of relationships and systems to better serve the needs of women and men and whole communities.

When we strive together to end the physical and emotional abuse of women, their economic insecurity and political powerlessness, their exclusion from decision-making processes, we ensure that women will be able to make their full contribution to every aspect of society. We work out of a faith commitment that proclaims that through Christ, a new humanity can be established for all persons in all places.

Rooted in the biblical accounts of the genesis of the world and the human family is the declaration that all persons, female and male, are created in the image of God, the giver of life. Human relationships have failed to mirror this imagery of creation in God's image, but women's experiences, their struggles for life and for nurturing life are crucial perspectives for safeguarding and liberating the creation.

The prophetic tradition calls the people of God to take on the task of living and working in solidarity with the oppressed to bring oppression to an end. Through our baptism we are incorporated into the body of Christ, the new community in which old patterns of relationships among classes, races and genders have been ended and new patterns are embodied that reflect the caring of the new age. Our call reminds us of the diversity of gifts that the Spirit imparts upon persons in the human family and the challenge to enable all persons to utilize those gifts for the building up of the community for justice and reconciliation in the world.

◇ **13** ◇

The Justice Agenda from the Inside Out

UNA KROLL

In the commentary that follows, British medical doctor Una Kroll presents in broad strokes the task of forging justice that lies ahead of us as we seek to be the church in solidarity with women. It is an ongoing task with many parts. Her statement can provide a framework for setting our justice agendas for many years to come.   *SC*

SOLIDARITY is a big word. To me it represents the following things:

- to value,

- to want justice for,

- to desire fulfillment for,

- to be willing to suffer for.

The church is called to be in solidarity with women inside and outside the church in a variety of ways.

Una Kroll is a deaconess of the Church of England and a medical doctor. She is the author of several books on women. This is an excerpt from a longer essay that first appeared in *Women in a Changing World*, a publication of the World Council of Churches, Geneva, June 1987.

Ways to Value Each Other

All member churches should be called on to value women as much as they value men, to find ways of expressing that fact, not in terms of role and function but in terms of personhood.

Within the churches this means encouraging men and women to find concrete ways of valuing each other for what they are and not simply for what they do biologically or socially.

Solidarity of the whole church with women in the church means in this context:

- Paying attention to language used in the liturgies about women.

- Paying attention to the way in which we stereotype women and men by the adjectives we use about each.

- Paying attention to the way in which we make value judgements about people according to the pronouns and adjectives we use about them. At first this has to be a self-conscious exercise; later it becomes spontaneous.

- Ensuring that we teach women about their value to the community and repeating that assurance many times by:

    - encouragement of talent,

    - recognition and serious consideration of women's opinions and ideas,

    - recognition and utilization of women's gifts.

Christian women who work outside the structures of the church's ministry in specialized ministries in the wider community should be shown that they are valued as much as those who work within the ecclesiastical structures by reward, being listened to, being shown that they are appreciated as valued colleagues.

Ways to Seek Social Justice

All churches should be called on to want justice for women in the community and in the church. In practice this means:

- Not being content that women are used exploitatively, as prostitutes, sexual objects, cheap laborers, expendable workers both inside and outside the home.

- Looking at their conditions of work inside the home and outside it to ensure that adequate remuneration is given for the work done for the whole community.

- Paying serious attention to the health of women and developing preventative and educational programs to teach women throughout the world about nutrition and health.

- Supporting women by word and deed when they are trying to secure economic justice. At present the majority of Western countries have a lamentable record of providing any support at all to Christian women who are in solidarity with their secular sisters in their struggles for justice in society. In my opinion this should be a priority for leaders to consider in all churches.

- Women outside the church will not take the churches seriously until women inside the church are both valued and supported in their persons, but it should also be said that the plight of women outside the church is much worse than that of most women inside the church, and all Christians should get their priorities right.

All churches should desire fulfillment for women, and a large part of that task consists in listening to what women want. In practice this means:

- Listening actively to single women, single parents, lesbian women, outcast women of all kinds. Providing support for women to listen to and work with outcast women.

- Ensuring by means of financial help that all women receive a good education, providing travel scholarships and educational resources for underprivileged women.

- Taking seriously women's ideas about what fulfillment means and not imposing men's ideas on women. I should like an audience of leading men in the church to be invited to listen attentively to what women have to say about this.

Christians in all churches should be prepared to suffer for women, not in the old patronizing chivalrous, "women and children first, God bless them," way but in real solidarity.

Whatever Gave Men the Idea...?

Whatever gave men the idea that women wanted to be protected, fought for and over, put over the sides of ships first in order to live on as widows? Women themselves might have other ideas altogether. Some might prefer to die alongside their men in times of war or when boats sink. Whatever gave men the idea that women would want to stay at home and cook and mend when their men were on picket lines, suffering hardship for principles, dying for their beliefs? Whatever gave anyone the idea that women were too weak to suffer and that they needed to be spared responsibility so that when the men in their family were all prematurely dead they could enjoy a penurious widowhood?

Surely to goodness it is time for men and women to rise up and say that these ideas may have been appropriate in a medieval society where many women died in order to populate our world but is wholly inappropriate in an overpopulated world where the best efforts of all people should be devoted to helping each other to remain alive, well and at peace with each other.

I feel very strongly about this, nay, passionately. In my opinion Christian men and women have not suffered with and for each other since the very early times of Christianity except in conditions where they find themselves on the same side of a real war. But I want Christian men and women to suffer with and for each other during times of peace and I want Christians to show the world what that kind of creative suffering can be like.

It is a sin for us in the Christian churches to be at war with each other in any way. It is also a sin to deny one sex the opportunity to suffer alongside the other sex. Together, using every talent and resource at our disposal, we should be striving to bring the good news of the gospel to the world. We should be working for peace. We should be working with each other and not against each other. We should know how to live with differences of opinion and we should stop all gender war, not invite one sex to do all the suffering and the other to take advantage of it.

Hence, if I want to say anything at all at this time to the churches, I want to invite them to make a serious study of how men and women *are* suffering together, and how they can suffer together creatively for the sake of the world, according to Christ's example.

The Holy Spirit Liberates and Unites

ARUNA GNANADASON

MY COUNTRY, India, is reeling under the drought that summer often brings with it. Some regions have waited for a year or even two for rain refuses to come. Women who live in the slums of Madras know the value of water. They are up at all times of the night and early morning in my city — even at 2:00 or 3:00 A.M. one can see queues of women trying to collect enough water from the common tap for their families. Clean drinking water is a rare commodity for millions of women in the South. The well itself is therefore a symbol of life.

The well and other watering places are places of community where women in India meet. They meet there to collect water, to chat with each other, to counsel each other and to take a moment of rest in the midst of their work-filled days. In this sense too the well is a symbol of life.

But it is also true that water sources have been the place of divisive tendencies in India. In a slum it could be a place of tension because every woman hopes to reach the tap before the water supply is discontinued. It is also here that the system of caste has found its most obvious expression. Dalits, the "out-castes" of Indian society, are denied the right to draw water from many wells and water ponds, even today. They are said to be "polluting" influences in upper-caste Hindu practice and thought. Where Dalits have had

Aruna Gnanadason is director of the World Council of Churches Subunit on Women in Church and Society. Reprinted from *Decade Link*, no. 9 (December 1991), a publication of the World Council of Churches, Geneva.

the courage to challenge this humiliating discrimination, they have been ruthlessly suppressed. Therefore while the well of water source is indeed a symbol of life, it cannot be ignored that it has also been a context of pain, tears, and hardship for women.

It is in this context that the encounter of Jesus with the Samaritan woman (John 4:5–30) comes alive to me. It takes place at a well — the source of life. Like women in India, this unnamed woman has to go outside the village to seek clean drinking water. She was a Samaritan woman — a Dalit of her time. In v. 9, we are told that Jews and Samaritans do not drink from the same vessels (see also 4:27). Samaritan women were considered a permanent contamination, as are Dalits today. Jesus does not only dialogue publicly with a woman whom any decent Jew would have shunned, but we see later that he also transforms this notorious sinner into his effective missionary to the Samaritans (4:28–30; 39–42).

Feminist theologians in India have been baffled by the time of day this event in Jesus' life takes place. The Bible clearly states that it is about the noon hour (v. 6). The sun must have been overhead, relentlessly beating down on this West Asian country — perhaps the reason why Jesus was thirsty for a drink of water. It is unusual for women to go to the well at noon. They normally choose a cooler time — early in the morning or in the late afternoon hour so as to avoid the heat. And yet, here was a woman making this journey at this unlikely hour, to collect water! She is alone — this is also unusual. Women normally go to the well in a group (see Gen. 24:13, where Abraham's servant seeks a wife for his master's son, Isaac, and chooses Rebecca). Perhaps it was because she was a Dalit, a Samaritan, and hoped to collect water when she would not be disturbed by women of other communities. Or perhaps she chose to get away briefly from a home environment, which Jesus refers to later (vv. 16–18).

Whatever the reason, the reality is that she is at the well and Jesus meets her there and asks her for a drink of water. She is shocked that Jesus, a Jew, a rabbi, and a male at that, asks her for water. Jesus then shares with her the promise of "living water." Perhaps in jest, the woman challenges him, saying that without a bucket or rope he would not be able to draw the water. Jesus tells her that the water at Jacob's well may temporarily quench her thirst, but the living water that he promises will give eternal life. This profound message of freedom and new life that Jesus shares with this simple woman is perhaps too confusing for her to understand totally, and her response sounds ludicrous and almost flippant, as we see in verse 15. In fact it is a normal response to expect from an overworked and burdened woman — she would welcome anything to reduce her labor. But if one strips away the outer layers of her response its real meaning becomes apparent. She yearns for this living water that will quench her thirst forever, so that she need not come regularly for water (v. 15). She soon realizes that this indeed is an encounter with the unusual — a man who perhaps can lift from her heavy heart the different forms of oppression that she experiences because she is a woman, a Samaritan woman at that, in very patriarchal and unjust times.

There is some controversy as to whether the next few verses (vv. 16–18) are part of the original manuscript or whether they are a later interpolation. Some scholars would hold that they are not part of the earlier text as their content does not really fit in with the rest of the passage. But these verses have to be understood in the perspective of a woman who is obviously bound by personal and structural sins of patriarchal control. She is indeed in need of the liberating power of the living water.

Jesus then proclaims, for the first time, that he is Jesus Christ, the expected Messiah. It is hard to understand why Jesus thought it fit to make this crucial announcement to a Samaritan, and a marginalized woman at that! Later in the passage we see that the disciples are astonished to find him talking to a woman (v. 27). Jesus throughout his earthly ministry broke barriers and ignored odious distinctions. St. Paul, therefore, speaks of the "in Christ" experience as a journey into a whole new world. It is not an individualistic, otherworldly or interior experience, but a new value system where the old and the accepted is broken down and a new, egalitarian and just community is realized.

To Jesus the "little ones" in society matter — the Samaritan woman's low position in society was not to keep her from sharing in the liberating power of the living water. Indeed, she deserved that. Jesus always chose the weak, the vulnerable — those who do not count in society, or rather, those who are told that they do not count. He takes them into his community and shares with them his message of freedom and hope. In the Jesus community — an ecclesia of equals — all those on the periphery find acceptance and love.

Worship in Spirit and Truth

It is important to note the dialogue the woman has with Jesus regarding worship (vv. 19–25). She refers to her ancestors, an Assyrian tribe from Samaria, and to their worship on the mountains. They were not able to totally reject their own gods and were therefore considered a "heathen" race needed yet to experience the saving power of the true God. Jesus points to the time when the Samaritans will recognize that God is spirit, and worship therefore must be in spirit and in truth. Christ shares with the Samaritan woman the promise of the Spirit as one "who accompanies, who helps, supports, advocates our causes — one who is an enabler," as Dr. Philip Potter reminded the World Council of Churches Assembly in Canberra. Christ seems to be foretelling that he will not be with the people of God forever — worship must be in spirit. But it will also be in truth. Later in John's Gospel (chaps. 14–16), the Spirit of Truth is described more fully: "What is the truth?," Pontius Pilate asks cynically. Dr. Potter told us that the "truth" in the New Testament is not an abstract word — it is that which is made open, made visible, uncovered, disclosed, that which becomes transparent. It is this truth that frees us, it is this that will free the woman of the well.

And yet the powerful ones in our societies have identified truth with the "knowledge" they have and used it as a weapon to manipulate others by ensuring that it is not available to all. The knowledge and wisdom of those on the underside of history have also been undermined.

Jesus' reference to the place of worship is important in this context as it meant something to the different peoples of his time. And yet he says in v. 21 that the point is not the place of worship, but worship that is in spirit and truth. As Christianity spread from a largely Euro-centered world, theological truth has been unduly influenced by the European cultural and value systems. Any new theological expressions, any attempt to articulate new theological paradigms based on people's experiences in other places and other cultures has been rejected as "syncretism"! Here Christ affirms that worship that is in spirit and in truth is true worship and the place from which it emerges is not important. The Spirit of truth speaks to different people in different ways. It demands not only mutual tolerance and respect, but each one's experience must be welcomed as a sign of the enrichment that comes to the whole church.

Jesus offers the Samaritan woman his promise of a new life — he calls her into a new relationship of acceptance and love, which obviously she does not enjoy in her familial and social situation. He gives her a new identity, a sense of "being" but also a sense of "becoming." She is called to receive the living water, the life-transforming message of freedom and hope, so that she will become heir to the liberating power of the Spirit of God.... The Samaritan woman too could become a child of God if she would worship in Spirit and in truth.

The Water Jar — A Past to Leave Behind

The Samaritan woman's first impulse when she receives the message of freedom is to leave her water jar behind (v. 28) and go into the town to share the good news that she has heard. The water jar is also a symbol of life to women — it is used to carry the water that sustains life for them and their families. In India women take great care to keep their water pots polished and clean, a shining symbol of their dependence on water sources for survival. Often the water pot is a woman's only expensive possession. The water jar could be seen as a sign of domestic slavery, but it could also symbolize women's intrinsic relation to the gifts of creation. It is therefore not usual for Indian women to use empty water pots in demonstrations demanding that the government provide them with clean water.

It is indeed strange that this woman in Samaria leaves her water pot behind in her excitement to take her people this startling message that perhaps she has met the Messiah! Her leaving of the water pot behind is proof of her determination to leave behind her life of oppression and sinfulness, so as to internalize the liberating power of the living water. The woman of Samaria had the courage to leave behind her oppressive familial and social situation. Perhaps we could stretch the image to see the water jar as a symbol of the empty "godless," selfish life that she is ready to leave behind. The living water has made her an heir and indeed a new creature.

The woman's first reaction to this strange new message, which obviously transforms her, is to be a missionary, an evangelist with a bursting message of hope to share with her people.

Perhaps she was now ready and impatient to confront and resist the forces of evil that oppressed her as a Samaritan woman. Jesus promises her the living water because he knows that before she can be a bearer of new life, she has to be cleansed of her complicity with her own subjugation and feelings of unworthiness (v. 9). Her attitude of self-abnegation, characteristic of many oppressed people, had to be thrown off.

There are many who would withdraw because they think they are too poor or too marginalized to experience the healing power. But Christ the Messiah (v. 30) is available and revealed to all — this is not the exclusive claim of a few!

The dialogue the woman has with Jesus is indicative of the conflict within her. She has to choose, either to walk with dignity and a consciousness of her own worth, leaving behind her old life as a despised Samaritan woman, or she can continue in what gives her apparent security within her community, however hateful it may be. If one chooses to be converted, one has the responsibility of bringing life to others. Conversion means getting involved in other people's lives. It involves a choice of either a self-less life for others or a self-centered but very comfortable and trouble-free individualism. What does this imply? Often we speak of conversion as a personal, saving experience that some privileged few can enjoy. But conversion must be a radical experience, one of confronting death in order to achieve resurrection. Getting involved in other people's lives means giving up some of the socio-economic privileges we have enjoyed and getting involved in the struggle of others. It cannot mean satisfaction with acts of charity, however sacrificial they may be. Conversion implies a form of rejection of the present. Where we see death at work, i.e., in the socio-economic injustices in this world cause poverty to many and allow a few to live a privileged, consumerist lifestyle. If conversion is what it should be — a change of outlook is imperative.

Elsa Tamez has written this about conversion:

> Conversion is a gift of God because it shows us the way and invites us to enter the world of freedom, the world of life. At the same time conversion is a human task, because it demands of us an individual and collective commitment to the building of that world.that

The conversion of the Samaritan woman demands all this of her.

Liberation Is a Process

Finally, Jesus makes clear to the Samaritan woman that the liberation she is to experience is not a once for all time experience — there is no magic water in the well that is going to liberate her for all times. She must constantly renew the liberation experience, not only by looking into her personal sinful life, but by sharing with other oppressed Samaritans like herself the promise of liberation.

This passage is rich with meaning, challenging us and leading us into a life of self-sacrificing witness in an unjust, divided world. But it also contains a promise: we are called like the Samaritan woman to a conversion experience into the Spirit that frees and unites.

THE MAGNIFICAT

And Mary said, "My soul magnifies the Lord,
  and my spirit rejoices in God my Savior,
for you, O God, have looked with favor on the lowliness
    of your servant.
  Surely, from now on all generations will call me blessed;
for you, O Mighty One, have done great things for me,
  and holy is your name.
Your mercy is for those who fear you
  from generation to generation.
You have shown strength with your arm;
You have scattered the proud in the thoughts of their hearts.
You have brought down the powerful from their thrones,
  and lifted up the lowly.
You have filled the hungry with good things
  and sent the rich away empty.
You have helped your servant Israel, in remembrance of your mercy.
according to the promise you have made to our ancestors
  to Abraham and to his descendants forever."*

In Advent of my first year as pastor, I read the Magnificat (Luke
1:46–55) one Sunday and was overcome by emotions. Before I got
much beyond "My soul doth magnify..." I was in tears and could
hardly continue. The thought that Mary's song was a woman's song,
a woman's prophecy, which for at least 1500 years women had been
forbidden to read in the officially sanctioned gatherings of public worship, was what did it. It felt so right and so exciting to be reading
this song in my own pulpit, where I had been freely chosen by these
people — a song about liberation, no less — that I began to weep. I
was, of course terribly embarrassed to do such a feminine thing, and
entirely surprised when members of the congregation began to reach
for their handkerchiefs. But I was even more determined to read the
whole passage, to enjoy the experience and not be prevented from
performing my duties as pastor, so, with long pauses for breath, I
proceeded to the very end of the New Testament reading. After that,
it got to be a sort of annual event. One Sunday in Advent, I would
read the Magnificat, and we'd weep just a bit.

> — From a program celebrating the experiences
> of women in ministry, compiled by Carol Ames

---

*NRSV text altered for inclusive language.

PART FOUR

The Promise:
There Will Come a Day

◇

The time is the last week of October 1991. I ponder how to end a book that has hardly begun to surface all the dimensions of its theme. On the TV evening news, Charlayne Hunter Gault is interviewing Hanan Ashrawi, that remarkable woman who is a member of the Palestinian delegation to the Middle East peace talks taking place in Madrid. I recall a comment made by one woman quoting another on past summit meetings. Celia Allison Hahn writes: "I look at those gathered...and see an ocean of dark flannel suits. The women are not there. As Ellen Goodman observed of news reports about the meeting: 'Women had no public role, so they were covered in their private role. Every item in each wardrobe was scrutinized....It is sad that the summit is one of the last bastions of an all-male world.'"[1]

Watching all the men representing Israel, Palestinians, Egypt, Jordan, Lebanon and Syria file into that grand hall in Madrid, I recalled past trips to the Middle East and life-changing conversations with

---

1. Celia Allison Hahn, "Men, Women, and the Remarriage of Public and Private Spheres," *Christian Century* (June 4–11, 1986): 550.

Middle East women — Israeli women, Palestinian women, Egyptian, Syrian, Jordanian, Lebanese women, and I thought, "If only the women were there." And then there appeared that one lone woman, Hanan Ashrawi. Strangely, for the next few days, she was the subject of my prayers — a kind of ongoing commentary addressed to God about what concerns me in any given day. And the image of Hanan Ashrawi kept coming to me. What a place for a woman. Would that she had at least one other woman as a co-delegate. Would that she had a counterpart, or two, on the Israeli side.

At any rate, she symbolizes as well as any image I could imagine today why the churches must be in solidarity with women. Women are needed in the public arena as much as in the private. We may not be better or wiser or more visionary than men, but we do bring a different perspective, when we are not co-opted by the male agenda. (And sometimes, a lone woman *is* co-opted because to stand apart, surrounded by male-only colleagues, is a very vulnerable place to be.) In our most visionary moments, however, women know the world is our home, and it is the place where all the world's children must live out their lives. Women *must* help shape its future.

When the Decade Ends

Will 1998, the end of the Decade of the Churches in Solidarity with Women, be a Year of Jubilee? Will we recognize changes in the way the church, male and female, lives out its faith, and the way it works in the world, that we can measure and celebrate?

Recalling some of the changes that have already happened, we can take heart. Many of us remember in our lifetime a past when:

- Mainstream Protestant denominations did not ordain women for ministry, nor did seminaries encourage them to enroll in the divinity programs. (They were encouraged instead to go into the "more practical" Christian education program.)

- There were no women bishops or heads of national or regional church offices, except in a few cases where women headed women's boards of mission.

- Women professors in seminaries were hard to come by.

- Women biblical scholars were unheard of.

- The idea of inclusive language was a laughing matter.

- The second-class treatment of female children and adults in church school curriculum, and all other media of the church, was the rule, not the exception.
- A feminist theology, a feminist hermeneutics, "Women-Church," women's spirituality — these were mostly obscure and unrealistic terms, known only to a few.
- Sexual harassment was not a matter to be taken seriously.
- Nor, for that matter, were equal employment opportunity, day care for children of working mothers or paid maternity leave.

And the list could go on. So, we *have* made progress. But what is our ultimate goal?

A few years ago, a Roman Catholic order of priests proposed that the Ten Commandments be recast as prophecy so that they might read: *"There will come a day when...* We will love our God. We will honor our fathers and our mothers. We will not murder." And so on. Suddenly, the commandments take on a totally new dimension of hope and promise.

If churches today were to express their dreams in the form of "There will come a day...," what would they sound like? Perhaps every local church could formulate its own set of hopes for men and women in solidarity with each other. A kind of random brainstorming might sound something like this:

There will come a day when:

- Each will see the other as created in God's image.
- Each will honor the other's gifts and find a way of benefiting from all those gifts.
- Some will preach and bear children as well.
- Some will prophesy and nurture children as well.
- Some will test the spirits.
- Some will prepare meals and serve them, as if they were serving the supper of communion.
- Some will clear the tables and wash the dishes, in the same manner.
- Some will teach, by example as well as word.
- Some will be advocates for the common good.
- Some will challenge the civic structures of the community to be just and fair in its treatment of all its citizens.

- Some will sit on the courts; some in the legislative halls of the nation.
- Some will raise our consciousness about the state of the world and our responsibility for righting wrongs.

(Add the ones you have thought of as you read this list.)

In all these and many other ways, we will seek the welfare of our community and the world. But we will not relegate home and private matters only to women, and civic and public matters only to men. "There are many members, yet one body" (1 Cor. 12:20, 26).

Return to Creation

To find a different way of being the church, however, is going to take much creative thinking and much hard work. Many of the old patterns will have to be rearranged and redesigned. This will be frightening to many because we are members of a body that claims an ultimate truth, given to us by God, handed down to us from one generation to another, but renewed in every generation by the work of the Spirit. How do we separate the ever-borning, living (animate) truth from all the inanimate household furnishings that have served us well in the past, but that now must be reconstructed, re-upholstered or relegated to the attic as antiques in the making? That is the question.

Perhaps it would help to compare the need for women to proclaim an interpretation of Christianity that makes sense for us to the need of Christians of other cultures to make Christianity "indigenous" to their own cultures. History has taught us that Western Christians made many mistakes in the past when we shared our faith with other peoples and other cultures and put too much pressure on new Christians to discard and deny all the ways and values of their traditions. Now Christians of other cultures are saying to us, "We did not have to give it all up. God had not left us totally without revelation, love, grace, the good gifts of creation prior to Christianity. We must see what God is doing in Jesus the Christ in the context of what God was already doing in our midst before we knew of Christ."

In other words, they are claiming the right to perceive and experience Christianity apart from its Westernization. In order for the faith to have its most significant impact on an Asian or an African culture, those cultures must perceive its witness in relation to their own reality.

In a similar way, women are saying that we must experience the faith not only through the eyes of the patriarchs, but through the eyes of the matriarchs as well as through our own experience of reality for it to have its most profound connection with our lives. Women know that they have experienced truth in the biblical tradition, even in the context of patriarchy. God has been immanent and available to us in every generation, even when the record keepers in the household of God did not totally grasp the extent of the evidence. But we also know that we perceive the faith in terms far beyond the limits of patriarchy. We must make the faith "indigenous" to our life as women.

SC

Bibliography

The resources listed here include some by authors whose articles appear in this book. But many books already mentioned in the text or footnotes are not repeated in this bibliography. For a more extensive listing, including audiovisual resources, see *Ours the Journey* (information on this study guide is given on the inside back cover).

The U.N. Convention to Eliminate Discrimination Against Women

The Convention on the Elimination of All Forms of Discrimination Against Women. New York: United Nations Information Office, UN Plaza, New York, NY 10017. The result of years of work by the U.N. Commission on the Status of Women, this international treaty has been ratified by over a hundred countries. The Convention spells out internationally accepted principles and standards for achieving equality between women and men, taking children and families into account as well.

A special booklet on "The Ratification of the Convention on the Elimination of All Forms of Discrimination Against Women" has been prepared by the Human Rights Office of the National Council of Churches, Room 634, 475 Riverside Drive, New York, NY 10115. Single copy, $1.50, which includes handling charges. Contains fact sheets, guides to discussion and a special liturgy pointing up the importance of ratification of the Convention, a step that the United States has not yet taken.

Resources on the Decade from the United States

The United States Office on the Ecumenical Decade of Churches in Solidarity with Women is staffed by Krista Hurty and is located at 475 Riverside Drive, Room 915, New York, NY 10115. (212) 870-2665. All World Council of Churches books related to the decade can be ordered through this office.

Ecumenical Decade 1988–1998, Churches in Solidarity with Women: Prayers and Poems; Songs and Stories. Geneva: WCC Publications, 1988. A rich collection of program resources, including the Decade poster. Third printing. $7.95.

Into Action...Resources for Participation in the Ecumenical Decade, Churches in Solidarity with Women, 1988–1998. $5.00 plus $3 for handling and shipping. Order #1522 from the U.S. Office of the Ecumenical Decade for Women, address above. Workbook and program resources for worship, presentations, proposals for social justice involvement, and stories from women on their experiences of a particular culture or religious tradition. A version is also available in Spanish.

Dios también me llama a mí: Recursos para la participación en la Década Ecuménica Iglesias en solidaridad con las mujeres, 1988–1998. The American Baptist Churches have published a book in Spanish celebrating and providing resources for the Ecumenical Decade. It is available from National Ministries, ABC, P.O. Box 851, Valley Forge, PA 19482-0851. Order #403-2-1971, $5.50.

Resources on the Decade from Canada

The Women's Inter-Church Council of Canada (WICC) is providing ongoing resources to the churches of Canada related to the Ecumenical Decade of the Churches in Solidarity with Women. For further information, write or call Vivian Harrower, Executive Director, 77 Charles Street, W., Toronto, Ontario, M5S 1K5. Telephone: (416) 922-6177. Samples of resources available from the Council:

"Resources on Family Violence from Church Denominations" lists resources recommended by the participating denominations, with description, price and ordering information.

WICC Newsletter, produced four times a year, provides information about issues of concern to women. A donation of at least $5 is requested.

Groundswell, published four times a year by the Canadian Ecumenical Decade Co-ordinating Group. Order from WICC, address above. A donation of $10 is requested. A forum for sharing creative ways to ensure that the goals of the decade are reached, nationally and internationally. It includes news, information, resources, ideas, and book reviews.

Resources Related to Themes of *We Belong Together*

Cannon, Katie G. *Black Womanist Ethics.* Atlanta: Scholars Press, 1988. A scholarly approach that explores the ethical values found in the history, literature and experience of black women in the U.S.

Cannon, Katie, Ada Maria Isasi-Diaz, Kwok Pui-lan and Letty Russell, eds. *Inheriting Our Mothers' Gardens: Feminist Theology in Third World Perspective.* Louisville: Westminster/John Knox, 1988. An ongoing dialogue of women from every continent who share their stories in the search for a theology that works for women in their variety of historical and social settings.

Chung, Hyun Kyung. *Struggle to Be the Sun Again: Introducing Asian Women's Theology.* Maryknoll, N.Y.: Orbis Books, 1990. The author, a noted speaker at the 1991 WCC Assembly, draws on stories, poems and theologies of Asian women as well as her own passion, anger and hope for survival, liberation and empowerment.

Eck, Diana L., and DeVaki Jain, eds. *Speaking of Faith: Global Perspectives on Women, Religion and Social Change.* Santa Cruz, Calif.: New Society Publishers, 1987. Voices of women from Asia, Africa, the Middle East and Latin America as well as North America and Europe — "seeking a common ethic and spirituality of social transformation," with a foreword by Rosemary Ruether.

Fabella, Virginia, M.M., and Mercy Oduyoye, eds. *With Passion and Compassion: Third World Women Doing Theology.* Maryknoll, N.Y.: Orbis Books, 1988. Essays from Latin America, Africa and Asia presenting theological thought from a women's perspective of poverty, oppression and biblical insight, advocating a liberating theology beyond gender embracing all humanity.

Fiorenza, Elisabeth Schüssler. *In Memory of Her: A Feminist Theological Reconstruction of Christian Origins.* New York: Crossroad, 1984. A scholarly egalitarian view of early Christianity, seeking to recover women's role; with commentary on basic biblical passages.

Fortune, Marie. *Is Nothing Sacred? When Sex Invades the Pastoral Relationship.* San Francisco: Harper & Row, 1989. Case study approach by a pioneer in working with congregations where members — most often women — have been victims of clergy sexual abuse.

Grant, Jacquelyn. *White Women's Christ and Black Women's Jesus: Feminist Christology and Womanist Response.* Atlanta: Scholars Press, 1989. An in-depth exploration of issues introduced by the author in her article in *We Belong Together.* Shows how a theology of liberation based on sexism alone ignores the experience of women of color and looks toward a theology that also takes seriously race and class.

Isasi-Diaz, Ada Maria, and Yolanda Tarango. *Hispanic Women: Prophetic Voice in the Church.* San Francisco: Harper & Row, 1988. Believing that what Hispanic women say and do is more important than their interpretation of it, the authors make lively use of quotes of women talking about their lives. Contents of each chapter are summarized in Spanish.

Mollenkott, Virginia Ramey. *The Divine Feminine: The Biblical Imagery of God as Female.* New York: Crossroad, 1983. This accessible book provides images of God as Mother Eagle, Nursing Mother, Female Homemaker, Midwife and Bakerwoman. The final chapter offers practical ways to use female imagery in worship while remaining faithful to the Bible.

Moltmann-Wendel, Elisabeth. *A Land Flowing with Milk and Honey: Perspectives on Feminist Theology.* New York: Crossroad. 1986. Deals with questions of women's self-discovery and a critique of traditional theology, with new perspectives on New Testament stories about women and Jesus.

Morton, Nelle. *The Journey Is Home.* Boston: Beacon Press, 1985. Autobiographical essays by a foremother, distinguished theologian, teacher and friend of many church women in leadership.

Nelson, James B. *Embodiment: An Approach to Sexuality and Christian Theology.* Minneapolis: Augsburg Fortress, 1979. Also *The Intimate Connection: Male Sexuality, Masculine Spirituality.* Louisville: Westminster/John Knox Press, 1988. Highly recommended by pastors and others who lead workshops in which men and women deal with issues of sexuality and faith.

Rebera, Ranjini, ed. *We Cannot Dream Alone.* Geneva: World Council of Churches, 1990. A collection of stories of women involved in projects designed to support development of rural and village women in some of the less developed areas of Africa, Asia, Latin America and the Pacific Islands. The title suggests the reason such projects need the support of the WCC.

Robins, Wendy S., ed. *Through the Eyes of a Woman: Bible Studies on the Experience of Women.* World YWCA. Geneva: WCC Publications, 1986. Also Wendy S. Robins and Musimbi R. A. Kanyoro, eds. *Speaking for Ourselves: Bible Studies and Discussion Starters by Women.* Geneva: WCC Publications, 1990. Excellent material for study groups or for reading on one's own. Focus is on voices and insights of women in many countries and situations.

Schaef, Anne Wilson. *Women's Reality.* Minneapolis: Winston Press, 1981. Still one of the best down-to-earth reflections on what it means to be female in a "white male society." By a psychotherapist who has led a number of seminars and workshops for church women. Men might also recognize their reality in relation to women by reading such a book.

Tamez, Elsa. *The Bible of the Oppressed.* Maryknoll, N.Y.: Orbis, 1982. Focuses on liberation from oppression as central to biblical faith. Also see Tamez's *Against Machismo.* New York: Crossroad, 1987).

Trible, Phyllis. *Texts of Terror: Literary-Feminist Readings of Biblical Narratives.* Philadelphia: Fortress Press, 1984. Walter Brueggemann writes of these readings, "She proposes to get the interpreter/expositor out of the way so that the unhindered text and the listening community can directly face each other." Texts include the stories of Hagar, Tamar, an Unnamed Woman and the Daughter of Jephtah.

Weems, Renita. *Just a Sister Away: A Womanist Vision of Women's Relationships in the Bible.* San Diego: LuraMedia, 1988. Retells and explores stories of biblical women through the African American oral storytelling tradition, describing how women feel about themselves and each other then and now.

Wren, Brian. *What Language Shall I Borrow? God Talk in Worship: A Male Response to Feminist Theology.* New York: Crossroad, 1989. A contemporary hymnwriter explores inclusive language and its underlying theology. He examines the positive implications for the whole church and especially for men seeking to move beyond patriarchy.

Acknowledgments

The editors are grateful for permission to reprint the following:

"Ordination from the Woman's Perspective," pages 76–89. From "Ministry of Word and Sacrament: Women and Changing Understandings of Ordination," by Barbara Brown Zikmund, reprinted from *The Presbyterian Predicament: Six Perspectives*, edited by Milton J. Coalter, John M. Mulder, and Louis B. Weeks. © 1990 Westminster/ John Knox Press. Reprinted by permission.

"Women, Word, and Song," 71–75. From *Birthings and Blessings: Liberating Worship Services for the Inclusive Church*, by Rosemary Catalano Mitchell and Gail Anderson Ricciuti. Copyright © 1991 by Rosemary Catalano Mitchell and Gail Anderson Ricciuti. Reprinted by permission of The Crossroad Publishing Company.

"A New Language of Prayer," pages 64–65. From *Prayers of Our Hearts in Word and Action*, by Vienna Cobb Anderson. Copyright © 1991 by Vienna Cobb Anderson. Reprinted by permission of The Crossroad Publishing Company.

Lines from the poem "Phenomenal Woman," by Maya Angelou, quoted on page 42. From *And Still I Rise*, by Maya Angelou. Copyright © 1978 by Maya Angelou. Reprinted by permission of Random House, Inc.

Quote on inclusive language by Browne Barr, page 63, Copyright 1988 Christian Century Foundation. Reprinted by permission from the April 13, 1988, issue of the *Christian Century*.

"The Pilgrim Bible," by Phyllis Trible, pages 15–17. From the *Auburn News*, Auburn Theological Seminary, New York, Spring 1988 issue. Reprinted by permission of the *Auburn News*.

"Where Hospitality Welcomes," by Susan Blaine, Robert Seaver and Janet Walton, pages 69–70. Reprinted by permission from *Let the People Worship*, vol. 3, Autumn 1988, The Schuyler Institute for Worship and the Arts, San Carlos, California.

"What Sins Should Women Confess?" by Valerie Saiving, pages 58–61. Reprinted from Valerie Saiving, "The Human Situation: A Feminine View," *Journal of Religion* 40, no. 2 (April 1960). Copyright © 1960 by The University of Chicago Press and used by permission of the Press.

"The Justice Agenda from the Inside Out," by Una Kroll, pages 112–115. From "Solidarity of the Church with Women," Una Kroll, In *Women in a Changing World*, no. 22, June 1987. Geneva, World Council of Churches. Used with permission.

"The Mind-Body Split," by Joy Bussert, pages 90–99. From *Battered Women: From a Theology of Suffering to an Ethic of Empowerment* (Minneapolis: Augsburg-Fortress, 1986). Used by permission of the author.

"Violence in the Parishes," by Mary Pellauer, p. 97. From Mary Pellauer, "Violence against Women: The Theological Dimension," *Christianity and Crisis* (May 30, 1983). Used by permission of Christianity and Crisis.

"The Holy Spirit Liberates and Unites," by Aruna Gnanadason, pages 116–121. Reprinted from *Decade Link*, no. 9 (December 1991), a publication of the World Council of Churches, Geneva. Used with permission.